Sunset

Children's Clothes & Toys

By the Editors of Sunset Books and Sunset Magazine

Lane Publishing Co. • Menlo Park, California

Book Editor:
Alice Rich Hallowell

Contributing Editor:
Holly Lyman Antolini

Design:
Lea Damiano Phelps

Illustrations:
Jacqueline Osborn

Photography:
Darrow M. Watt

Photo Editor:
JoAnn Masaoka

Acknowledgments

Our thanks to the many designers and home sewers who generously shared their time and talents with us. We are particularly grateful to Ellen H. Ahrbeck for her thoughtful critique of the manuscript, and to Cynthia Overbeck Bix, Karen Cummings, Phyllis Dunstan, and Heidi Merry for their editorial contributions. We also extend special thanks to Concord Fabrics, Lynne B. Morrall, Sara Robb, and Myrna Wacknov.

Cover: A bright beanbag chicken makes a whimsical steed for this little girl and her child-size doll. You'll find instructions for the chicken on page 90, for the doll on page 80. Other projects shown include the doll's quilted jacket (page 62), our model's appliquéd bears and heart pin (page 43), and a pair of sock dolls (page 72).

Editor, Sunset Books: David E. Clark
First printing October 1983

Contents

Children's Clothes

Techniques, embellishments, projects

Countless are the ways you can enhance a child's garment to make it special. This chapter is chock-full of ideas to use on the next garment you make, buy, or rejuvenate.

Consult "Techniques," pages 5–23, for valuable hints on the basics, such as how to make clothes that grow with your child. And look to "Embellishments" on pages 24–57 for ways to dress up fabric—appliqué, Seminole patchwork, painting, and more. Step-by-step projects on pages 58–63 tell you how to make some extra special clothing items, from first snip to last stitch.

Techniques

Here's an abundance of ideas—both practical and pleasing—on how to handle the basic ins and outs of sewing clothes for children. It seems formidable at first to deal with all the little bits of fabric, tiny corners, and tinier fasteners. But with the following tips and instructions at your fingertips, you'll soon discover that children's clothes can be amazingly easy to sew.

On the following pages, you'll find sewing techniques to use as you make a garment from a pattern. You'll also find suggestions, whenever possible, for using the same techniques on completed garments that need some work.

The following information will take you from the basics of measuring your child and determining the correct pattern size (see "Measuring up," page 7), to such helpful techniques as simplifying seams (see "Seams," page 16). Especially important for children's clothes are techniques for adding room to grow (see "Making clothes that grow," pages 10–13), as are ideas on how to cover seam lines once growth tucks and hems are released (see "Operation coverup," page 13, and "Ruffles & strips," page 11), and many more.

With all this information at your fingertips, you'll find "Techniques" a good reference section to consult whenever you start a new project or rejuvenate an old one.

The emphasis in this book is on the needs and tastes of children ranging from infants to preschoolers.

INFANT: newborn to 6 months
TODDLER: 6 months to 2½ years
PRESCHOOLER: 2½ years to 6 years

Pattern selection

It's difficult to keep up with children's sizes—during their first few years, children seem to grow faster than you can blink an eye, and staying one step ahead of their clothing needs isn't easy.

Cut the challenge down to size by choosing patterns with simple lines and easy directions. Then decorate these garments with lots of trims or colorful embellishments to make them special and fun (see "Embellishments," starting on page 24).

Below are some pattern-selection hints that apply to all children's clothes. You'll also find some special features to look for, corresponding to your child's stage of development and needs. Keep these ideas in mind when you shop for garment patterns.

Basic guidelines

Children's wear is ideal for the sewing novice—most designs are simple, little fitting is required, and youngsters won't notice any mistakes you may make while mastering a technique.

Whatever your level of expertise, remembering these hints will help you get the most from each pattern you purchase.

● There must be plenty of room throughout a garment for ease of movement, without its being droopy or baggy. For example, drop shoulder or kimono sleeves are comfortable and unrestrictive, and accommodate lots of growth (**Ill. 1**).

Ill. 1

Roomy pants legs with elasticized hems allow room for running without the hazard of tripping (**Ill. 2**).

Ill. 2

● Details are important to consider. For example, shoulder straps should crisscross in the back of a garment so they won't fall off the shoulder. For further support, an epaulet or strap at the shirt shoulder will moor the strap in place.

Avoid using bows to tie garments at the shoulders. They may look pretty at first, but they untie all too quickly and are difficult for the young to manipulate.

● To allow for rapid growth, look for patterns that already (or can be easily altered to) include growth tucks, adjustable straps, and elasticized waistbands.

● Look for patterns with options for variety, such as blouses with several variations, or pants with short and long legs or various hem treatments. Also keep in mind the variety you can get by embellishing a simple garment. The plainest dress comes to life with the addition of some ribbons, buttons, or appliqués.

You can use one pattern over and over again, with no one the wiser, if each version has its own personality (**Ill. 3**). A big fringe benefit is that you become familiar with a pattern as you reuse it, and you can make each garment a little faster than the time before. Or you can make several

For little treasures

This simple purse can win any little girl's heart, and it's small enough to make with leftover fabric scraps.

You'll need: Scrap fabric, interfacing, ¼″-wide double fold bias tape, 1 yard narrow ribbon, 3 appliqués, 1 snap or 1″ strip of nylon self-gripping fastener.

● Step 1. Enlarge pattern; cut two A and one B from fabric. Cut one A from interfacing. Sandwiching interfacing between fabric layers, baste A pieces, *wrong* sides together.

● Step 2. Stitch bias tape over straight edge of piece B. Then baste B, *right* side up, to bottom half of A to make pocket of purse. Pin bias tape around outer edge of purse; turn under ends of tape and overlap them ¼″; stitch in place. Fold purse along foldline; press.

● Step 3. Use ribbon for shoulder strap; stitch ends at dots on back of purse. Stitch appliqués over ends of straps.

● Step 4. Fasten purse flap with the snap or self-gripping fastener. Cover fastener stitching with third appliqué.

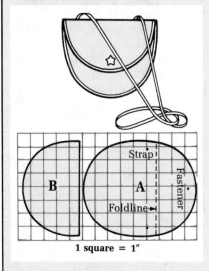

1 square = 1″

. . . Pattern selection

versions at once, assembly-line fashion, for the ultimate in efficiency.

Ill. 3

● Look for patterns that transcend seasons. Can you make the garment in different weights of fabric? Are there long sleeves and short sleeves? Are there pieces to add for layers of warmth? Though kids grow quickly, you can use one pattern to cover two seasons if the garment is adaptable.

Playclothes should be easy to make and tough to wear out, but there's always a need for a special party outfit. Since dressy clothes aren't worn frequently, they're the place for intricate details and pretty fabrics. By incorporating growth tucks (see "Making clothes that grow," starting on page 10), you can afford the time to make an exquisite garment, knowing that it can last for several years, or several children.

Changing needs

As children grow and develop from infants to toddlers to preschoolers, their abilities and their resulting clothing needs change dramatically. Awareness of these needs will help you provide a wardrobe that's attractive and functional.

Infants. Infants are pretty restricted in movement for the first few months of their lives. Warmth and comfort are the most important clothing considerations at this time.

Sleepers with feet or closable bottoms are the most in demand, since they keep babies warm when the covers are kicked off.

Choose front-opening garments with easy access to the baby's diaper. Make sure slip-over garments fit easily over the head. Don't let fasteners get too small or too numerous—it's hard to button lots of tiny buttons on a squirming baby.

Toddlers. Still in diapers, toddlers require clothes that are easy to change. Look for snaps at the crotch and legs of pants, or elasticized waists in pants and skirts.

Coveralls are a good choice for toddlers who are crawling and learning to walk; they protect the legs and don't ride up while the toddler's in motion.

Older toddlers and preschoolers. Playclothes are necessities for these age groups. Choose patterns that encourage physical activity; avoid designs that restrict movement. Even dressy clothes should be comfortable.

As toddlers learn to manipulate small objects and coordinate their movements, they'll want to dress themselves (though undressing is their forte!). By the middle of the preschooler years, children are able to dress themselves independently.

To help children in this learning process, choose patterns for pull-on clothes or clothes with front openings that are easily seen and reached. Keep the number of fasteners to a minimum. (See "Fasteners" on pages 20–21 for further details.)

Measuring up

Children come in all shapes and sizes, just as adults do. Body measurements—rather than age —are the best indicators of the correct pattern size needed for a child. Update these measurements each time you shop for patterns, since children grow quickly.

When you're looking for children's patterns, you'll notice that many designs are interchangeable for boys and girls. Boys' bodies are at the same stage of development as girls' from infancy through preschool.

Size ranges

Each pattern company has its own sizing system; look for size and measurement charts at the back of each pattern catalog. Though sizes are fairly standard among pattern manufacturers, they do vary in the Infant or Baby sizing categories; check the charts carefully before you buy a pattern.

Infants. Baby or Infant pattern sizes are designed for babies not yet able to walk. Since movement is limited for a young child, fitting clothing to exact body dimensions isn't necessary. Use height and weight measurements to determine pattern sizes at this stage.

Toddlers. Toddler pattern sizes are designed for a figure between a baby's and a child's.

Some Toddler sizes seem to overlap into the Children's size range. The important difference between the two is the diaper allowance provided in Toddler sizes. In addition, the Toddler dresses are shorter than a similar Child's dress.

In this size range, the chest, waist, and height measurements

are the most important. If there's a disparity between your child's measurements and those on the manufacturer's chart, use the child's chest measurement instead of height as a guideline for shirts, jackets, or dresses. Likewise, use the waist measurement for pants and skirts; it's easier to alter the length of a garment than the width (see "Altering" on page 8).

Preschoolers. Preschoolers move from Toddler sizes into Children's sizes. Children's pattern sizes reflect a widening back and shoulder dimension. They're narrower than Toddler patterns through the waist and hips because they no longer provide room for diapers.

In addition to waist, chest, and height measurements, you'll need to record your child's back waist length, hip, and crotch measurements.

Taking measurements

As you take each measurement, hold the measuring tape snug, but not tight. Take children's measurements over their underwear, including diapers (**Ill. 1**).

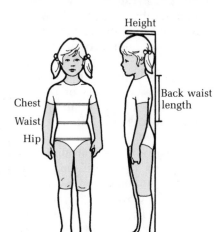

Ill. 1

Getting a child to hold still long enough for you to take accurate measurements can be a challenge—but you can try making a game of it.

Because a child's waistline is hard to locate, tie a string around the child's middle and have the child bend or twist from side to side as if doing calisthenics (**Ill. 2**). This movement shifts the string to the natural waistline.

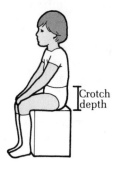

Ill. 2

To take an accurate crotch depth measurement, sit the child on a flat surface and measure the distance from the child's waistline to the surface (**Ill. 3**).

Ill. 3

Altering

It's hard to imagine how quickly a child can grow. But right before your very eyes, those plump round bodies stretch out long and lanky. During their first six years, children grow up much more rapidly than they grow out, so alterations for height are more common than those for width.

Lengthen or shorten

If your child's back waist or height measurements differ from the pattern size, adjust the pattern at the pattern adjustment lines, or at the hem.

If your child's measurements differ from your pattern only in the back waist, alter the pattern in the bodice on any garment with a waistline, such as a dress, a jumpsuit, or overalls. If height is the problem, adjust the hemline or the pattern adjustment lines below the waist. Instructions follow.

Remember to repeat any alterations on the *back* of the garment as well as the front. If you've altered the length of a garment in an area with buttons, carefully respace the button and buttonhole markings so the spaces between buttons are equidistant.

The bottom line. If the pattern's hemline is relatively straight, shorten the garment's length by carefully redrawing the cutting line. To lengthen, tape tissue paper to the hem edge and redraw the cutting line to the desired length.

Inside lines. When the pattern's hemline curves, or you want to alter the length in another specific area of the garment, find the pattern's lengthen/shorten adjustment lines—they run perpendicular to the grainline.

Shorten the pattern piece by measuring up the desired amount from the adjustment line; draw a line across the pattern piece. Make a fold on the adjustment line and bring the fold up to the drawn line; tape in place. Carefully redraw the pattern cutting lines (**Ill. 1**).

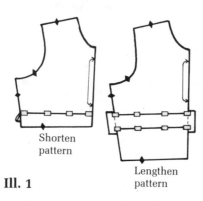

Shorten pattern

Lengthen pattern

Ill. 1

Lengthen pattern pieces by cutting across the adjustment line and spreading the two pieces evenly over tissue paper. Tape both pattern pieces in place on the tissue paper; carefully redraw the cutting lines (**Ill. 1**).

Widening seam allowances

This is a good technique to use on clothes without waistline seams. It adds extra fabric to the side seams to allow you to widen the garment later, prolonging the garment's life.

Increase the pattern side seams, sleeve facings, or underarm seams by ¼ inch. These measurements add 1 inch to the total garment width.

Construct the garment according to the all-in-one side seam method on page 19. Stitch a ⅞-inch-wide seam.

When it's time to widen the garment, restitch the seams ⅝ inch or ½ inch from the edge; remove the original stitching.

all-in-one side seam method on page 19.

Glossary

Here you'll find definitions and illustrations of sewing terms used throughout this book.

Bias
The diagonal line formed by folding the fabric so the crosswise threads run parallel to the selvage.

Fabric cut along the bias is very stretchy—helpful when you want fabrics to follow a curve.

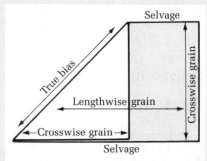

Double-stitched seam
An all-in-one seam and seam finish used on sheer fabrics, lace, and fabrics that tend to curl at the edges, such as knits.

Sew a plain seam. Then stitch another row within the seam allowance, ¼ inch from the first row, using either a straight or zigzag stitch. Trim seam allowance.

Ease stitch
A type of gathering stitch that eases a longer fabric edge so it fits against a shorter one to make a seam without showing gathers. This allows extra room for movement in areas such as shoulder and elbow seams.

Stitch ⅛ inch outside the seamline on the longer piece, between the ease marks using long machine stitches. Pin the garment pieces together; pull the thread to distribute the gathers evenly. Stitch the seam without catching gathers.

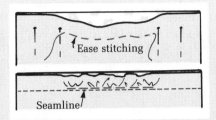

Ease stitching

Seamline

Edgestitch
A straight line of functional or decorative stitching, close to the edge of the fabric. Stitch the fabric, *right* side up, ⅛ inch to ¹⁄₁₆ inch from the edge of the fabric.

Graded seam
Seam allowances trimmed to different widths to minimize bulk. Use in areas such as facings, where both seam allowances are pressed to one side.

Trim the seam allowance that will lie against the fabric to ⅜ inch. Trim the remaining seam allowance to ¼ inch.

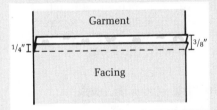

Garment

¼" ⅜"

Facing

Narrow hem
To sew a narrow hem, turn the raw edge under ¼ inch; press. Turn under ¼ inch again; press. Machine stitch close to the edge.

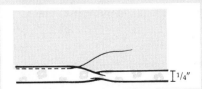

¼"

Slipstitch
An invisible hand stitch used to join two pieces of fabric in a

seam, or to stitch a flat hem on the wrong side of the garment.

On seams, pick up one fabric thread with your needle. Do the same on the opposite fabric, about ¼ inch forward. Pull the thread taut.

On hems, pick up one fabric thread alongside the hem edge. Then take a stitch through the top of the folded hem edge.

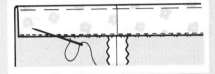

Stab stitch
A stitch technique used primarily for embroidery.

Inserting the needle perpendicular to the fabric, pull the thread completely to the *wrong* side before bringing the needle back up to the surface.

Stab stitch

Staystitch
To prevent garment pieces from stretching out of shape during garment construction.

Before sewing the garment, stitch all the curved or bias-cut edges of each garment piece in the seam allowance, ¼ inch from the seamline, using the stitch length you'll use for seams.

Stitch-in-the-ditch
Stitching through a seam so that no stitches are visible on the

right side of the fabric. This technique is used when you turn a cuff, waistband, collar, or facing and stitch its underside to the garment's *wrong* side at the seamline.

To do so, stitch through the seam from the *right* side of the fabric, spreading the fabric on either side of the seamline as much as possible so as to place each stitch in the seam itself.

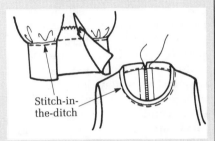

Stitch-in-the-ditch

Understitching
A row of stitching to prevent seams from rolling to the outside of the garment edge, especially on facings and collars.

Press the seam allowances and facing or undercollar away from the garment; pin in place. With the *right* side up, stitch close to the seamline through the facing and seam allowances.

To understitch a collar, stitch only along the outer edge of the collar. Start and finish the stitching about 1 inch from the collar points; it's impossible to get the presser foot any closer to the point.

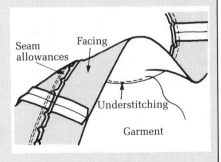

Seam allowances

Facing

Understitching

Garment

Making clothes that grow

Children are notorious for growing quickly—seemingly before your eyes. Clothes that fit them one day seem to have shrunk the next. To get the most wear out of the children's clothes you make, either add growth features as you make them, or plan attractive ways to lengthen the garments later.

Before adding any growth features to a garment you're making, assess the value of the effort. Consider the life expectancy of a particular garment with respect to your child's rate of growth and activity level. Crawling toddlers and climbing preschoolers often wear out their playclothes before they outgrow them. The most likely candidates for growth features are dressy clothes and sturdy, long-wearing garments such as overalls.

Fabrics best suited to growth features are light to medium-weight ones that wear well, are colorfast, and won't show scars where stitches are removed. Avoid napped fabrics, which may become crushed and marked by stitching and wear.

To make the release of growth features as simple as possible, use a long machine stitch when you sew the growth tuck. On inside tucks, use a slightly different color of thread that clearly contrasts with construction seams inside the garment.

Here are some simple ideas for prolonging a garment's usefulness:

• Plan to increase length eventually by adding a ruffle or a patchwork strip to a hem edge.

• Make slightly deeper hem and wider side seam allowances than usual, then let them out later.

• Make shoulder straps longer, and reposition the strap buttons as length is needed.

Inside growth tuck

Hidden behind a hem, an inside growth tuck can add as much as 2 inches of length to a garment. And by using the technique below, you can let out the tuck without removing the hem stitching.

Plan to make the finished tuck ½ inch to 2 inches deep and at least ½ inch shorter than the hem allowance so it won't peek out beneath the garment's edge. For example, **Ill. 1** shows a common 3-inch hem allowance accommodating a 2-inch tuck. Releasing the tuck increases the garment length by the depth of the finished tuck.

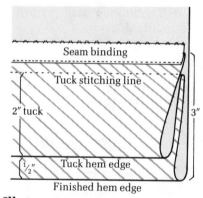

Seam binding
Tuck stitching line
2" tuck
3"
½"
Tuck hem edge
Finished hem edge

Ill. 1

Begin by modifying your front and back pattern pieces to accommodate the tuck: tape tissue paper to the bottom edge of each piece.

Determine the finished hem length and mark it on the pattern tissue. Add the depth of the hem allowance plus twice the finished tuck depth (the additional length needed to make the tuck). Use the total to determine the bottom edge of the unhemmed garment, measuring down from the finished-length mark; then mark the bottom edge on the tissue. Extend the pattern side edges to the new bottom edge.

Cut the fabric garment pieces and mark tuck foldlines on the *right* side of the fabric as shown in **Ill. 2**, measuring up from the bottom of each piece.

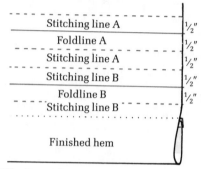

Stitching line A — ½"
Foldline A — ½"
Stitching line A — ½"
Stitching line B — ½"
Foldline B — ½"
Stitching line B
Finished hem

Ill. 2

After constructing the garment, turn under the finished hem edge; press. Make the growth tuck by folding the hem allowance along the tuck foldline, *wrong sides together*; press.

Align the tuck foldline with the appropriate throat plate guideline for the desired finished tuck depth; stitch the tuck. Press the tuck toward the hemline; proceed with the hem.

Outside growth tuck

You can decorate a garment as well as create extra room for growth by adding outside growth tucks (**Ill. 3**). Place one to three rows of these horizontal outside tucks just above the hem, waistline, or sleeve hem. The tucks can be ⅛ inch to 1 inch deep.

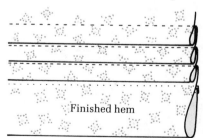

Finished hem

Ill. 3

A ½-inch tuck will add 1 inch to a garment's length when it's released. You can release each tuck separately as needed without removing the hem.

Begin by lengthening your front and back pattern pieces with tissue paper and marking the bottom edge as explained under "Inside growth tucks," allowing twice the finished depth of each tuck you intend to add along with the hem allowance.

For tucks on sleeves, cut across the sleeve pattern 1 inch above the bottom edge and insert a piece of tissue paper as described under "Bodice tuck." Keep the tucks very narrow (⅛ inch to ¼ inch).

For tucks above the waist, add extra length to the body of the bodice pattern and keep the tucks ¼ inch to ¾ inch deep.

After cutting the fabric garment pieces, mark tuck foldlines on the *right* side of the fabric as shown in **Ill. 4**, measuring up from the bottom of each piece and making sure the bottom tuck is positioned high enough not to interfere with a hem or seam. **Ill. 3** shows three ½-inch tucks.

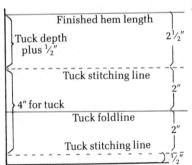

Finished hem length	
Tuck depth plus ½"	2½"
Tuck stitching line	
4" for tuck	2"
Tuck foldline	
Tuck stitching line	2"
	2½"

Ill. 4

Construct the garment and proceed with the hem. Fold, press, and stitch the tucks, as described for "Inside growth tuck." Press the tucks toward the hem.

(Continued on page 12)

Ruffles & strips

Suddenly there's a lot of leg showing beneath the edges of clothes that are practically new. If there's no more hem to let down, help clothes keep up with the child by adding some ruffles, or a fabric insert. Whichever device you use, repeat it elsewhere on the garment to lend credibility to the ruse.

First aid station

Tattered knees and flapping pockets; vexing rips and defiant stains—sound familiar? Maybe too familiar? Despair no longer. Here are some suggestions for reinforcing and repairing children's clothes.

Reinforcements. For the major areas of concern—knees, elbows, and pockets—take action to avoid problems before they occur. Reinforce stress points as the garment is being made or when it's fresh from the store.

If your child is especially hard on pockets, see "Pick a pocket" on page 18 for reinforcing hints. Or baste folded pieces of seam binding under pocket corners on the *wrong* side of the garment to prolong pocket life.

Reinforce knee and elbow areas by making a patch of lightweight fabric interfacing for extra durability. To cover a knee, make it large enough to stretch from the inseam to the outside seam of a pants leg; stitch it into the garment seams against the fabric's *wrong* side. For an elbow, sew a patch to the *wrong* side of the garment in the vulnerable area (or use fusible interfacing and fuse it in place, if you don't want stitches to show).

Patches. Outside patches are a fun, bright way to perk up clothing while repairing or reinforcing worn-out spots. Be adventurous and creative: play with colors and fabric types and shapes—patches don't have to be square to be functional.

Whatever the style and location of a decorative patch, make sure it coordinates with the garment in some way. Use patches of fabric from coordinating garments or accessories, or carry your cover-up technique to other parts of the garment for a pulled-together look. On the knees, use a fabric that matches the shirt; cover a tear with an appliqué that's repeated around the skirt or up on the sleeve. Hand or machine embroider a design over a small patch, and continue the needlework in a pattern on the garment. Then the clothes are not only repaired—they take on a whole new personality.

For added protection and dimension, quilt the patch fabric or pad the patch with a layer of polyester fleece. For durability and extra strength, zigzag stitch around the outside edge of the patch through the garment fabric, and stitch again inside the first row of stitching.

Bodice tucks

An inside or outside tuck at the waist of a garment allows room to grow between the shoulder and the waist (**Ill. 5**). A finished bodice tuck can be up to ¾ inch deep, adding twice its depth or up to 1½ inches of length when released. You can add this tuck on the inside or outside of a garment at the natural waistline.

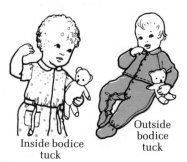

Inside bodice tuck

Outside bodice tuck

Ill. 5

To place a growth tuck in a bodice, first modify your front and back pattern pieces. Draw a line across the pattern piece, perpendicular to the center front or back line, 1 inch above the waist seamline. Cut along the drawn line and insert a piece of tissue paper. Keeping the original waist size, redraw the side seams.

After cutting the fabric garment pieces, mark tuck foldlines as shown in **Ill. 6**, measuring up from the waistline seam. Mark the lines on the *right* side of the fabric for an *outside* tuck, and on the *wrong* side for an *inside* tuck.

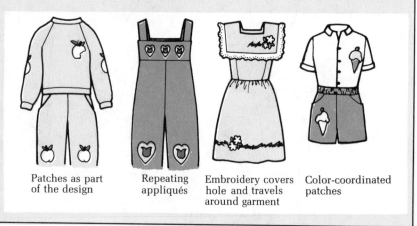

Patches as part of the design

Repeating appliqués

Embroidery covers hole and travels around garment

Color-coordinated patches

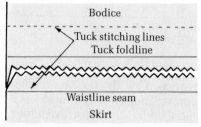

Bodice

Tuck stitching lines
Tuck foldline

Waistline seam

Skirt

Ill. 6

After stitching the waistline seam and before installing the zipper or other fasteners, fold and press the fabric along the tuck foldline, *right* sides together if the tuck is *inside*, *wrong* sides together if the tuck is *outside*. With the waistline seam allowances held out of the way, stitch the tuck just above the original waistline seam, as described for "Inside growth tuck," above (**Ill. 7**). Press the seam and tuck toward the bodice; insert the zipper.

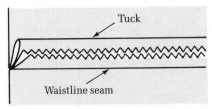

Ill. 7

When you release this tuck you'll have to release and restitch the bottom of the zipper.

Shoulder tucks

You can create two or three ⅛-inch to ¼-inch-deep vertical tucks on each shoulder of a garment. These tucks are *release tucks*: rather than running the full length of a garment piece, the stitching stops so that the tuck opens at the bottom, releasing fullness. They will add ½ to 1½ inches of fullness in the chest area and allow an increase in breadth across the shoulders later. The tucks can be stitched on the inside or the outside of the garment (**Ill. 8**).

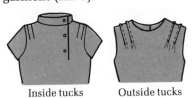

Inside tucks   Outside tucks

Ill. 8

Alter the front and back bodice pattern pieces by drawing a line down from the center of the shoulder on each piece, perpendicular to the shoulder seam and stopping even with the center of the armhole (**Ill. 9**). Next, draw a second line at a right angle from the bottom of the first line to the armhole edge. Cut along the drawn lines and spread the two pieces on tissue paper as shown in **Ill. 9**, until the shoulder seam line is opened the distance needed to accommodate the shoulder tucks: twice the total depth of all the finished tucks. (For example, two ¼-inch tucks will require a 1-inch spread.) Redraw the shoulder seam.

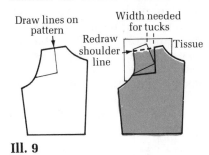

Draw lines on pattern   Width needed for tucks   Redraw shoulder line   Tissue

Ill. 9

Perpendicular to the shoulder seam, draw 2-inch-long tuck foldlines on the front and back pattern pieces. For tucks stitched on the *inside* of the garment, mark the tuck foldlines on the *wrong* side of the fabric. For tucks on the *outside*, mark the foldlines on the *right* side. Foldlines should be equidistant from the center of the shoulder. All foldlines should be spaced so that the stitching of adjoining tucks will not overlap.

Stitch the shoulder seams; press open. For inside tucks, fold and press the garment, *right* sides together, on the tuck foldline; stitch the tucks, as directed for "Inside growth tuck," above. For outside tucks, fold and press the garment, *wrong* sides together, and stitch.

Operation cover-up

When hemlines are lowered and growth tucks released, wear marks, stitch marks, and crease lines may be evident. If so, it's time for creative cover-ups.

Don't approach this task as simply a patching mission. To make your camouflage effective, expand your thinking to include more than just a one-line cover-up. Instead of one row of rickrack to cover a crease line, use three or more rows, experiment with different sizes or colors, and even mix in some other trims. Laces, braid, ruching, or strips of patchwork are all great solutions.

Divert attention to other parts of the garment as well as the portion you're covering, to make the design look well planned and balanced. For example, after covering hem or shoulder tuck lines, carry the theme—or a hint of it—to other areas, such as pockets, sleeves, yokes, or waistbands. A little planning like this can result in a great rejuvenation.

The final touch

The next time you give a handmade gift, delight child and parent by attaching a personalized gift tag. It adds an extra touch of *you*, making a gift very special.

Ideas abound, both functional and fun. For example, a garment tag that provides care instructions and includes an extra button or two is a most appreciated gesture.

A toy takes on its own personality when you add a card that provides the name and "biography" of this new friend. A short, whimsical story is sure to capture the fancy of its receiver and make the gift endearing.

Let the design of the tag reflect the personality of the gift or the event being celebrated—try a birthday-present tag shaped like a birthday cake or a clutch of balloons.

Imitate the shape of the gift itself, or something you'd associate with it. For example, tag a teddy bear with a honey pot or a paw print. A shirt with a stenciled design can have a similarly stenciled tag, or a tag cut in the stencil shape.

If handmade gifts become a habit, you might want to design a standard tag that represents you and your craft. A sewing machine, spool of thread, or pair of scissors will clue everyone in.

Tucks

To lend a touch of crisp neatness to a garment, take some tucks. Tucks are small folds of fabric, stitched in place. Some patterns feature them as part of the garment design; if not, you can add them yourself for a new look.

Vertical tucks can be stitched the full length of garment pieces such as those for a bodice or sleeve. Or they can be stitched a short way and left open at the bottom, releasing fullness and allowing room for future growth. The latter type—known as a release tuck—is discussed under "Shoulder tucks" on page 13.

There are three types of tucks: *blind tucks, spaced tucks,* and *pin tucks* (**Ill. 1**). Blind tucks overlap each other, each concealing the stitching of the next. Spaced tucks are separated by spaces of fabric. Pin tucks are very narrow—usually ⅛ inch deep or less; they may be either blind or spaced.

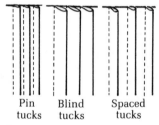

Pin   Blind   Spaced
tucks   tucks   tucks

Ill. 1

To introduce vertical tucks to a flat pattern, stitch the tucks into the fabric before cutting the pattern pieces. Begin by estimating how much yardage you'll need: multiply the number of tucks by twice the finished tuck depth and add this measurement to the pattern width.

When you're ready to stitch the tucks, mark their foldlines on the *right* side of the fabric along the fabric grainline. Fold the fabric, *wrong* sides together, along the foldlines; press. Align each tuck foldline with the appropriate throat plate guideline for the desired finished tuck depth (or if the tuck is deeper than the available guidelines, place a piece of masking tape to use as a guideline); stitch the tuck.

Position the pattern pieces over the tucked fabric with the pattern grainline arrow parallel to the tuck lines (**Ill. 2**). Proceed as the pattern directs.

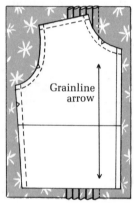

Grainline arrow

Ill. 2

Scalloped tucks. To impart a delicate and old-fashioned air to a party outfit or to embellish a christening gown, you might add some *scalloped tucks.*

To construct a scalloped tuck, stitch a ¼-inch-deep tuck. Mark ½-inch intervals and make scallops by taking two overhand stitches in each spot and pulling each taut (**Ill. 3**). Conceal the thread between the scallops by drawing it through the inside of the tuck.

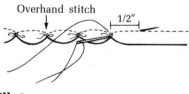

Overhand stitch   1/2"

Ill. 3

Ruffles

Ruffles are one of the most feminine touches you can add to a child's outfit. Rows upon rows of them make any little girl feel like a princess. Even a pair of corduroy overalls becomes dainty when a simple ruffle is added.

A ruffle is a strip of fabric, cut two to three times longer than the finished ruffle's length and then gathered to fit the garment. The fabric weight and the size of the ruffle determine the amount of fullness you'll need. Sheers and lightweight fabrics need extra fullness for body; heavy fabrics are gathered with less fullness, to avoid bulk and weight. Deep ruffles need more gathering than shallow ones to look full.

There are two basic types of ruffles: ruffles stitched into a garment seam or onto a raw edge, and freestanding ruffles with headings, stitched to a garment surface.

Ruffles can appear at any seam or raw edge. Try adding them at necklines, cuffs, or hems, down the front edge of a blouse, or in a yoke seam. Ruffles also add a pleasing touch to the side seam of pants, on the outside edge of shoulder straps, around the edges of a vest, or in tiers on a skirt.

Ruffle in a seam

Once you've decided to add a ruffle to a seam or edge of a garment, you can choose to finish its bottom edge with a narrow hem or a self-faced hem. The finish you select determines the amount of fabric you'll need.

Narrow-hemmed ruffle. A narrow hem requires the least fabric and is best suited to light to medium-weight fabrics. To determine the dimensions of the

strip of fabric for a ruffle with this finish, measure the length of the seam or edge to which the ruffle will be attached and multiply it 2 to 3 times, depending on the desired fullness of the ruffle. If you wish to use bias fabric for a softer look, see "Cutting bias strips" on page 32. Then determine the depth of the ruffle by adding 1⅛ inch for the hem and seam allowance to the desired finished depth.

Stitch a narrow hem at the bottom edge of the ruffle; continue with "Gathering and stitching," below.

Self-faced ruffle. To make a self-faced ruffle, follow the directions for the "Narrow-hemmed ruffle," doubling the desired finished depth and adding two seam allowances to obtain the ruffle's depth dimension. Fold the fabric in half lengthwise with *wrong* sides together; pin in place. Gather both layers as one.

Gathering and stitching. Make two rows of long machine stitching—gathering threads—within the seam allowance (½ inch and ⅜ inch from the raw edge of a ⅝ inch seam); don't backstitch. With *right* sides together, pin the ruffle to the garment in equal increments, leaving the ruffle fabric loose between pins.

Secure the gathering threads at one end. At the other, pull the bobbin threads until the ruffle fits snugly against the garment, adjusting the gathers until they are even. Then secure the loose ends of the gathering threads.

Pin the ruffle in place at frequent intervals to maintain the adjustment (**Ill. 1**). Stitch the seam, if the ruffle is attached to a raw edge. If the ruffle is inserted in a seam, stitch the garment according to pattern directions.

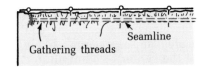

Gathering threads   Seamline

Ill. 1

Ruffle with a heading

A ruffle with a heading is a decorative ruffle stitched directly to the *right* side of a garment, forming two ruffles in one.

Cut or piece together a strip of fabric the desired finished depth of the ruffle, including the upper and lower ruffles, plus ½ inch for hemming. To determine the length, follow the directions under "Narrow-hemmed ruffle," above. Turn both raw edges under and stitch a narrow hem in each; then stitch two rows of long machine stitching, ½ inch apart, at your chosen line of division between the two ruffles (see "Gathering and stitching," above).

To attach the ruffle to the garment, mark a line on the garment to use as a placement guideline. Pin the *wrong* side of the ruffle in equal increments to the *right* side of the garment, matching the guideline to the ruffle division line. Adjust the gathers as directed in "Gathering and stitching," above. With the ruffle facing up, topstitch just outside each gathering line. Carefully remove the gathering stitches (**Ill. 2**).

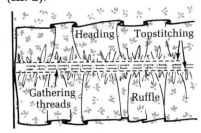

Heading   Topstitching

Gathering threads   Ruffle

Ill. 2

Seams

When your child shows off the marvelous new garment you've made, the seams aren't likely to be the center of admiration. Yet that wonderful new outfit could be very short-lived without a careful choice of seam type. The finished seam in a child's garment must be smooth and pliable for comfort, but sturdy enough to withstand hard wear and frequent washing.

If you sew a plain seam in a garment, it is wise to add some reinforcement to ensure its durability.

• Strengthen the seam by topstitching: press both seam allowances to one side and topstitch through all layers, ¼ inch from the seamline.

• On knit fabrics, prevent seam allowances from curling by stitching a second seam in the seam allowance, ⅛ inch from the seamline. Trim the seam allowance close to the stitching.

Below, you'll find some less familiar seam techniques that are excellent choices for children's clothes, though they might not be described in your pattern guidesheet.

Flat-fell seam

The flat-fell seam creates a sturdy finish that will withstand hard wear and frequent washing, making it the perfect choice for your youngster's hard-working playclothes and sleepwear. It adapts well to straight or slightly curved seams and suits all but the heaviest of fabrics.

To make a flat-fell seam, stitch the seam with the *wrong* sides of the fabric together; press the seam open and then to one side. Trim the bottom seam allowance ⅛ inch from the stitch-

ing (**Ill. 1**). Fold the top seam allowance in half as shown. Pin it in place over the bottom seam allowance; edgestitch it to the underlying fabric.

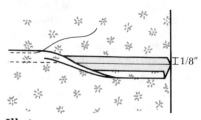

Ill. 1

French seam

The French seam is strong and easy to stitch, and leaves no raw edges to ravel or to irritate delicate skin. It's especially good for sheer fabrics, on which seams are visible. The French seam works well on straight seams, but it's not recommended for curves or sharp corners.

To construct a French seam (**Ill. 2**), stitch a ⅜-inch seam with the fabric's *wrong* sides together. Trim the seam allowances to ⅛ inch from the stitching; press the seam open. Now turn the fabric and fold it so the *right* sides are together, using the seam you just completed as the foldline. Stitch ¼ inch away from the fold, enclosing the raw edges. Press the seam to one side.

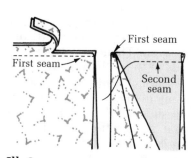

First seam
First seam
Second seam

Ill. 2

Taped seam

For a decorative finish, you can encase seam allowances in bias tape to make a taped seam. Reverse the garment, and you see the seamline centered between two rows of topstitching. It's a great way to take care of bulky, raveling, or quilted fabrics, as well as reversible or unlined garments. Choose bias tape in matching or contrasting colors or patterns (or see page 32 to make your own).

Inside taped seam. Construct the garment according to pattern directions. Trim the seam allowances to ¼ inch; press open. If your fabric is quilted, reduce its bulk by cutting out exposed batting.

Fold the bias tape in half and press a crease down the center. Align the bias tape over the open seam, centering the crease over the stitching (**Ill. 3**). Baste the tape in place to ensure that the stitching which will show on the reverse side of the garment will be even. Then edgestitch (see page 9) down each side of the bias tape. Remove the basting threads.

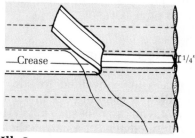

Crease

Ill. 3

Outside taped seam. Construct the garment with the seam allowances exposed on the *right* side by stitching the pieces with the *wrong* sides together; continue as described above.

Facings

Little clothes have little facings—and you may find them more than a little difficult to handle. When the neck and armhole facings in your pattern are too small to manipulate, replace them with either a combination facing or a self-bias casing.

No matter what type of facing you use, select the fabric carefully and use the tips under "Facing finishes" to ensure successful results.

Fabric selection. Since facings should be flat and invisible from the *right* side of the garment, the weight of the fabric used for the facing is of prime importance. With light to medium-weight fabrics, use the same fabric or fabric weight for the facing as for the garment. With heavier fabrics or pile fabrics, reduce bulk by choosing a facing fabric of lighter weight and tight weave.

Though only your child will know, it can be fun to make the hidden facings in a contrasting color or print, to add a very special secret touch to a garment.

Combination facing

You can easily combine your pattern's separate neck and armhole facings into one piece, called a *combination facing.* The combination facing eliminates the exasperation of handling many small pieces in a small area, and also reduces bulk. The bit of effort you spend making a new pattern piece is a small price to pay for the ease of handling it provides.

Make a pattern for a combination facing by placing tissue paper over the garment pattern and tracing the existing armhole, shoulder, and neck lines (**Ill. 1**). Then, following each side seam allowance edge, draw a 2-inch

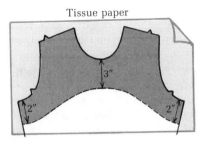

Tissue paper

3"
2"   2"

Ill. 1

line down from the armhole.

Mark a point 3 inches down from the center of the neckline. Connect the center point with the two side lines, using a curved line as shown. The curve must arc in this manner to ensure freedom of movement in the chest and shoulder areas. Make a pattern for both the front and back of the garment.

Join the front and back facings at the shoulder seam and finish the lower facing edge according to pattern directions. With *right* sides together, stitch the facing to the bodice at the neck and armhole seamlines.

Turn the garment *right* side out by reaching through the space between the facing and garment shoulder and pulling the garment back through the space (**Ill. 2**). Lift the facing away from the garment and stitch the side seam in one continuous seam; press open. Proceed as the pattern directs.

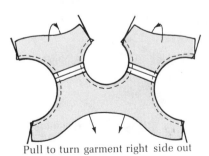

Pull to turn garment right side out

Ill. 2

Facing finishes

Whether you use the facings supplied with your pattern or decide to make the combination facing, it helps to take some precautionary measures to prevent unsightly rolling or bulging at the facing edges. Follow these hints for professional results.

● Trim 1/16 inch from the neck and armhole edges of facing pieces before attaching them to the garment. Because the facing is now slightly smaller than the garment, the garment fabric will roll in slightly rather than the facing rolling out.

● Avoid the bulk problem posed by heavy fabrics: simply finish the facing edges by overcast stitching or by binding them with bias tape (see page 32).

● After sewing facings to a garment, remember not only to trim, but also to grade the seams, leaving the widest seam allowance against the garment.

● Finish facing seams with understitching to prevent the facing from rolling to the outside of the garment.

Self-bias casing

You can eliminate facings altogether by binding raw edges with bias tape. This makes a simple, attractive finish for necklines and armholes as well as cuffs and hems, and is an ideal way to reduce the bulk of heavy or quilted fabrics.

First, trim the garment seam allowance of the area to be bound 1/4 inch from the seamline. Cut a length of bias tape 2 inches longer than the area to be bound. To install it, follow the instructions in "Encasing a raw edge" on page 33.

Pick a pocket

Pockets are places for tucking treasures or parking hands, and sometimes just for looking pretty.

For extra strength and durability, line or interface pockets. In addition, reinforce pocket edges by stitching a small triangle or square or zigzag stitching a ½-inch-long bar tack at each upper corner. Double stitching the pocket in place adds strength, too.

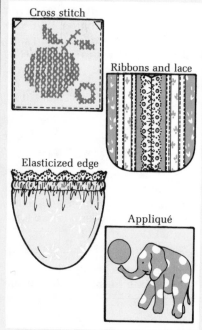

Cross stitch

Ribbons and lace

Elasticized edge

Appliqué

Possibilities for enhancing a patch pocket are limitless: change a basic U or square shape into a heart, half-circle, or pleated cargo pocket shape. Add a flap or an elasticized opening. Trim the pocket with buttons or tucks. Cut the pocket fabric on the bias, quilt it, add a trapunto or appliqué design, or embroider it.

Decorative trims add special touches to pockets. Add ribbon, rickrack, eyelet ruffle, piping, or colorful topstitching across the top or around the edges of pockets.

Collars

You can perk up a seemingly ordinary collar in countless ways. Simply using a different fabric color or texture is a good start.

A touch of trim calls special attention to any collar. At the outer edge of the collar, use piping, lace, or a fabric ruffle to add appeal. Follow the collar shape with a line of rickrack, soutache braid, or narrow ribbon. Add spice with rows of decorative stitchery.

Eliminating the collar altogether is another option. Try a simple bias-bound neckline instead (see page 33) or attach a ready-made lace collar. Knit collars and cuffs can be purchased in kits to add to a knit shirt.

Collar construction tricks

Here are some helpful ideas to use when you're making a collar.

● Keep an undercollar invisible and help the collar maintain its roll by trimming ¹⁄₁₆ inch from the outer edges of the undercollar before stitching the collar pieces together. Understitching is another way to guarantee a perfect collar edge.

● Reinforce collar points by using small stitches—at least 12 stitches to the inch—near the points (**Ill. 1**). Instead of pivoting at the points, take 2 or 3 stitches diagonally across each point, as shown. You'll discover that the points are much easier to turn and they won't open up.

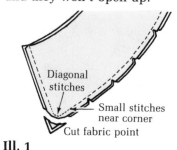

Diagonal stitches

Small stitches near corner

Cut fabric point

Ill. 1

Knit neck

A few inches of knit ribbing are all you need to convert a knit shirt pattern into a turtleneck or crewneck style. It makes an easy pull-on shirt for youngsters who like to dress all by themselves.

To determine the dimensions of the ribbing you'll need for a collar, double the desired finished collar height and add 1¼ inches for seam allowances. This will be the width of your ribbing piece, measured parallel to the ribs of the knit. Next, determine the length you'll need by folding the ribbing in half lengthwise—perpendicular to the ribs of the knit—and stretching it around your child's head, making sure it isn't too snug. To this measurement, add 1 inch for seams; then cut the ribbing.

With right sides together, stitch the narrow ends of the ribbing together ½ inch from the edge. Fold the band in half lengthwise, *wrong* sides together. Divide its circumference into four equal sections with the seam as one division; mark the divisions with pins. Divide the neckline in the same manner.

Pin the band to the garment neckline with right sides together, matching quarter marks and aligning the ribbing seam with a shoulder seam (**Ill. 2**). With the collar on top, stitch the collar and garment together ⅝ inch from the edge, stretching the collar to match the neckline as you go. Trim close to the stitching, then proceed with the pattern as directed.

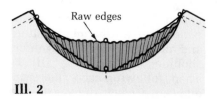

Raw edges

Ill. 2

Sleeves

Children's sleeves present problems from top to bottom. At the top is the arduous task of stitching tiny armhole seams. A simple bypass method will make the job easier. At the bottom is the challenge of providing hem variety. That's easily met with one of the elasticized cuffs below. Or try binding sleeve edges with bias tape for soft appeal (see page 33) or adding knit cuffs to knit sleeves (see "Knit neck" on the facing page).

Flat seam sleeve attachment

Do you wince at the thought of stitching tiny sleeves into tinier armholes? Try this technique: stitch the sleeve cap to the armhole before stitching the side seams or sleeve seams. It's remarkably manageable.

Finish the garment shoulder seams and neck edge according to pattern directions; don't stitch the side seams. Gather the sleeve cap if directed by your pattern, but don't stitch the underarm seam. With wrong sides together, stitch the sleeve cap to the armhole; stitch a second row ¼ inch away from the first, in the seam allowance (**Ill. 1**).

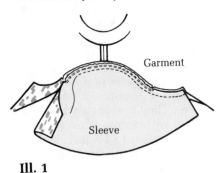

Ill. 1

Pin the side seam and underarm seam and stitch this edge in a continuous seam from the garment's bottom edge to the

sleeve's bottom edge (**Ill. 2**). To make a smoother and stronger curve as you round the armhole seam, make a small diagonal stitching line instead of pivoting the fabric.

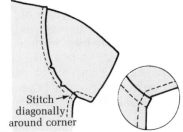

Ill. 2

Elasticized sleeve hems

You can add elastic to the hem of a full sleeve or substitute it for a cuff on a gathered sleeve. Or position the elastic slightly higher so it leaves a ruffle at the edge.

Hem with self-casing. To make a self-casing, re-mark the pattern by measuring ¾ inch below the sleeve's finished hemline (if your hem allowance is only ½ inch, you'll need to add tissue paper to the bottom of the sleeve pattern). Draw a line and use it as your new cutting line.

Wrap ¼-inch elastic around the child's arm at the point the cuff will touch. Make sure the elastic fits comfortably without pinching; add an extra ½ inch for overlap, and cut the elastic.

Stitch the sleeve's underarm seam. Tack down any seam allowances within the casing area to make it easier to pull the elastic through the casing. Turn the sleeve's bottom edge under ¼ inch; press. Turn it under again, ½ inch; pin in place. Stitch the upturned hem edge to the sleeve, leaving a 1-inch opening for the elastic. Edgestitch along the bottom edge (**Ill. 3**).

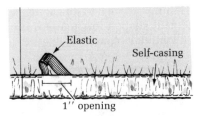

Ill. 3

Insert the elastic through the opening. Overlap the elastic ends ½ inch and stitch them together; stitch the casing opening closed.

Ruffled hem with self-facing. To add a simple ruffle at the wrist, follow the directions above for "Hem with self-casing," adding twice the desired ruffle depth to the ¾ inch you allow below the finished hemline. (For example, to make a 1-inch ruffle, you'll add 2¾ inches below the pattern's hemline.) It's best to make the finished ruffle at least ½ inch deep.

Cut the elastic and stitch the underarm seam as directed under "Hem with self-casing." Turn the sleeve's bottom edge under ¼ inch; press. Turn it under again, the depth of the ruffle plus ½ inch (1½ inches for a 1-inch ruffle); pin in place.

Stitch the upturned hem edge to the sleeve, leaving a 1-inch opening for the elastic (**Ill. 4**). Stitch again ½ inch below the upturned edge. Insert the elastic and close the casing as directed under "Hem with self-casing."

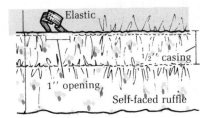

Ill. 4

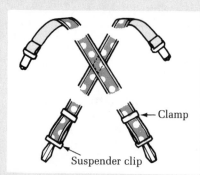
Fasteners

Dress infants with ease and encourage youngsters to dress themselves by simplifying the task with handy fasteners. Look for patterns with fasteners on the front of the garment, where they can be easily seen and reached.

Toddlers 2 to 3 years old are eager to dress themselves and can manipulate large buttons. By the time they're 3 to 4 years old, they can completely dress themselves—provided the fasteners are in front.

Buttons

Buttons are a source of endless fascination for little children. There's a limitless assortment of decorative buttons to choose from (see "Buttons for fun" on the facing page).

The two basic types of buttons are those with shanks and those without. If you're using a flat, shankless button, make a thread shank to prevent strain on the fabric. When the fabric is sheer or the buttons purely decorative, no shank is needed.

To make a thread shank, choose a pin, toothpick, or matchstick equivalent to the desired shank thickness (the thickness of the garment plus ⅛ inch) to use as a spacer. Place the spacer on top of the button as you sew the button to the fabric, stitching through the button and over the spacer (**Ill. 1**).

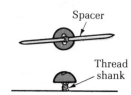

Spacer

Thread shank

Ill. 1

When the button's secured, remove the spacer. Pull the button away from the garment until

the stitches are taut. Wrap the thread end several times tightly around the stitches under the button to make the shank; secure the thread end (**Ill. 1**).

You can also make a thread shank on your sewing machine, using the spacer technique outlined above and following your machine manual's instructions on button stitching.

Zippers

Zip—it's open! Zip—it's closed! What could be more mesmerizing than a zipper? Those with large pull tabs are especially easy to manage, and encourage children to dress themselves.

Choose a zipper with the weight and flexibility to match your garment fabric. If a zipper will lie against the skin, use a nylon type rather than a metal one.

Shorten zippers by whipstitching across the zipper teeth at the determined length and cutting off any excess zipper tape ½ inch below the stitches.

Nylon self-gripping fasteners

As you make your child's garment, nylon self-gripping fasteners—also known as hook and loop tape—may be practical substitutes for buttons and snaps. They're simple to stitch in place, and they open and close quickly—a boon in dressing babies. They're also easy for little fingers to operate. This type of fastener tends to be stiff; it isn't suitable for use with sheer fabrics or in long strips.

Hook and loop fasteners are available by the yard in strips of various widths, or in precut geometric shapes. Some have an adhesive backing for self-basting.

To install hook and loop tape, position the tape along the garment center front lines, or the center of the marking where the original fastener was to appear (**Ill. 2**). Place the loop half of the tape on the upper side of the underlap and stitch around the outer edges through all layers. Place the hook half on the underside of the overlap and stitch as you did the first half.

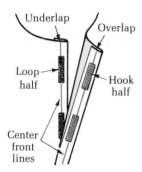

Ill. 2

Snaps

Snaps are especially good closures for infants' and toddlers' sleepers, T-shirts, and rompers. They're available individually or on cloth tape you can purchase by the yard (**Ill. 3**).

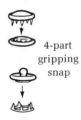

4-part gripping snap

Ill. 3

A decorative four-part snap is simple to install without special equipment. Follow the manufacturer's instructions, adding interfacing as directed to reinforce any areas of lightweight fabric that need it.

Buttons for fun

Buttons do more than hold a garment closed: they decorate! So many imaginative buttons are available—bright red hearts, cheerful ducks, gingerbread men, even alligators. Why not put them on your children's clothes just for fun?

Try new and surprising places for buttons: on a waistband, down the front of a T-shirt, on a sleeve, or on a pocket.

Hems

The home stretch: when the hem is done, the outfit is ready to wear! Whether you're creating a new garment, adapting a hand-me-down, or taking up a gift that's a bit too long, the same principles of hemming apply.

The tendency is to make a child's hem as deep as possible to allow for growth. But the depth of a hem should be determined by the style of the garment and the weight of the fabric, so keep these guidelines in mind:

Make plain, straight hems as deep as 3 inches. Make flared hems with fullness in the hem allowance no deeper than 2 inches. For a garment such as a circular skirt, make the hem only 1 inch deep. Use narrow, machine-stitched hems for blouses and shirts. Avoid wide hems if the fabric is heavy or bulky.

To hem quilted fabrics, trim the batting from the hem allowance (you'll have to remove some quilting stitches to do this) and stitch the hem by hand or machine. Or cut the hem allowance away and encase the raw edge with bias binding (see page 33).

Machine-stitched hems

Machine-stitched hems are the best choice for children's clothes because of their strength and durability, not to mention the fact that they're done in a jiffy. Machine stitching is suitable for all fabrics except those that are heavy or napped.

Topstitched hem. Topstitching finishes a hemming job quickly and adds a decorative touch to the garment's edge. Use a long straight stitch or try one of your machine's decorative stitches for an irresistible accent (see pages 24–25). (Remember, though, that decorative stitches are difficult

to remove if you want to let the hem down later.)

Turn the raw edge of woven fabrics under ¼ to ½ inch before turning the hem edge, to prevent raveling (this isn't necessary for knits). Turn the hem edge under and pin or baste it in place. Stitch on the right side of the garment, securing the hem and the turned edge with one or more evenly spaced rows of stitches. On knit garments, cut away any excess fabric above the topstitching to within ¼ inch of the top row of stitching (**Ill. 1**).

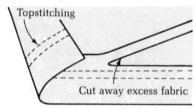

Topstitching

Cut away excess fabric

Ill. 1

Repeat the rows of stitching elsewhere (on the sleeve hem, at the neck, or at the waistline) to unify the garment's design (**Ill. 2**).

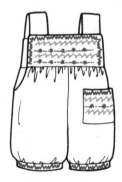

Ill. 2

Blind hem. The machine blindstitch is a strong finish that's barely visible on the outside of the garment. Most zigzag machines are programmed to stitch a blind hem (**Ill. 3**). Check your

machine's manual for specific instructions.

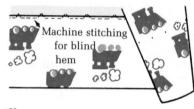

Machine stitching for blind hem

Ill. 3

Hand-stitched hems

Hand-stitched hems are usually reserved for special-occasion clothes on which a soft, invisible hem is desired. They also provide a smooth finish for heavy or napped fabric. Here are some tips to keep in mind as you hand stitch hems for your children's clothes.

If the garment shape flares at the hem, you'll need to reduce the fullness in the hem allowance. First, ease stitch (see page 8) with a long machine stitch ¼ inch from the raw edge; adjust the fullness at frequent intervals. Then place a press cloth between the hem and the garment to prevent a hem imprint on the front of the garment. With an iron, steam the hem to shrink out any excess fullness.

To stitch the hem on a lightweight or sheer fabric, precede the hand stitching by folding the raw edge under ¼ inch and machine stitching close to the fold. Pin the hem in place and secure it with a blindstitch.

Before hand stitching, prepare a fabric that tends to ravel: machine stitch ¼ inch from the raw edge. Pink close to the stitching. Pin the hem in place and secure it with a blindstitch.

Another way to prepare loosely woven fabrics for hand

stitching is to finish the edge with seam binding (on a straight hem) or bias tape (on a flared one). If the fabric is heavy, fold the taped edge forward and blindstitch the inside hem edge to the garment (**Ill. 4**), to avoid creating a crease on the garment's right side.

Heavy fabric

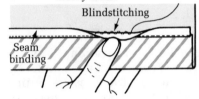

Ill. 4

Removing a hem

Once you've removed stitches to let down a hem, you may find a telltale sign of the original hem in the form of a soil line, persistent crease, or wear line.

If the hemline is creased, sponge it with a solution made of equal parts of white vinegar and water. If the crease stubbornly refuses to disappear, steam it by sandwiching the hemline between two damp press cloths lined with aluminum foil on the outside, and pressing it with a hot, dry iron.

If a line persists, you can disguise it in any of several imaginative ways—see page 13 for ideas. Whatever decorative finish you decide to add, make it compatible with the garment style and fabric and, if possible, repeat it elsewhere on the garment for harmony and symmetry.

Away with stains

Along with a child comes the inevitable problem of stains. It's amazing the number of messy things a child can get into! Below is a chart that deals with the most bothersome stains, giving quick and easy ways to remove them. (Except where otherwise specified, the treatments are for washable fabrics. If yours is nonwashable and no technique is given, have the stain removed by the dry cleaner.)

There are two basic rules for stain removal: First, be sure to treat a stain promptly. Then launder or dry clean the item immediately after treatment.

Most common stains respond to pretreatment with a commercial enzyme presoak, followed by laundering.

Here are definitions of some cleaning terms:

● Freezing: Hardening the staining substance by pressing an ice cube on it.

● Presoaking: Placing the stained fabric in water or a solution containing a stain-removal agent for a specific time. Follow by laundering.

● Pretreating: Rubbing an enzyme presoak or a liquid detergent into the stain.

● Scraping: Gently using a dull knife or spatula to remove the staining substance.

STAINS	TREATMENT
Blood	Sponge or soak stain immediately in cold water. If stain remains, pretreat it with an enzyme presoak. Sponge nonwashable items with a mild solution of detergent and water.
Chocolate	Sponge promptly with cold water (for tougher stains, soak in cold water at least 30 minutes). Rub with a detergent; rinse. If stain persists, sponge remaining stain with a cleaning fluid.
Crayon/Cosmetics	Sponge liquid detergent over stain, rubbing until suds are produced. When stain is no longer visible, rinse thoroughly. Repeat until stain is gone. For nonwashable items, sponge repeatedly with a cleaning fluid.
Egg	Scrape off as much as possible and sponge with cold water. Avoid hot water at all costs; it will set the stain permanently.
Fruit & juice	Soak immediately in cool water. (If stain is old, soak in hot water.)
Grass (foliage, flowers)	Sponge with rubbing alcohol to remove the stain from washable and nonwashable items; test colors first, and dilute if necessary. (Don't use on acrylic.) If stain persists, rub with detergent.
Gum	Freeze until gum is hard, then scrape it from fabric. If stain remains, sponge with a cleaning fluid.

Embellishments

Turn a simple garment into a prized possession: just add a touch of trim or stitchery. Boys and girls are thrilled to have their clothes decorated with their favorite objects or scenes.

From machine stitchery to fabric paint, you'll find in this section a treasure chest full of ideas to make your projects one of a kind. Whether you've just dabbled in the fabric arts, or have logged many years with a needle and thread, these instructions will help you create magical effects with the clothing you make.

Though the following embellishments are easier to execute on the flat fabric before you construct a garment, all of them—except smocking—are transferable to completed clothes.

As you browse through this section, let your imagination inspire you to develop ideas for design, color, and technique. Large illustrations throughout the chapter present these fabric crafts, translated into clothing for boys and girls—adapt their ideas to your child's personal preferences. "How to transfer a design," page 38, offers several ways to move your design from paper to fabric.

Decorative machine stitching

Your sewing machine is the key to a treasure trove of decorative stitching ideas. All you need are some brightly colored threads—the machine will transform them into marvelous decorations.

You can use programmed stitches or freehand embroidery to decorate garments you're making or clothes you've bought. Machine-stitched decorations are also ideal for touching up worn clothes; hiding hemline marks, stains, and small tears; or just giving a face lift.

Programmed stitching

Most sewing machines have at least one or two stitches that can be used decoratively. Such decorative stitches are either built into a machine's functions or programmed with the addition of a cam or cassette. Use them in single or multiple rows, mixing stitch designs and thread colors.

Decorative stitching is very becoming in any number of spots: around the edge of a collar or on the narrow bib of a pair of overalls or a pinafore, for example (Ill. 1).

Ill. 1

Use it to sew a machine-stitched hem, creating instant enhancement. You can also work your way up from the hem of a skirt, pants, or sleeves with many horizontal rows of stitches (Ill. 2).

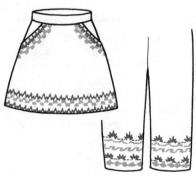

Ill. 2

Machine preparation. Consult your sewing machine manual for specific instructions regarding the features on your machine and any preparation needed for the stitch you've chosen.

Try different thread varieties for your upper thread, to create special effects. Lightweight thread makes a small stitch very delicate; machine buttonhole twist adds a bold appearance; and metallic thread makes a dazzling accent (Ill. 3).

Intricate stitch with fine thread

Open stitch with heavy thread

Ill. 3

Freehand machine embroidery

Master the technique of moving an embroidery hoop under your sewing machine needle, and you can create a limitless variety of freehand embroidered designs, including monograms. Adding the same delightful personal touch as hand embroidery, machine-embroidered designs are faster to complete and more durable.

This technique requires practice and familiarity with the handling of your machine. Experiment with several test samples to get used to hoop movements and a fast machine speed, and to become accomplished at making smooth, even stitches.

Fabric preparation. Create your design on paper first. Begin with simple shapes and move to more complex ones as you become more proficient at your embroidering technique. Transfer your design to the *right* side of the fabric (see "How to transfer a design," page 38).

For napped fabrics, such as terrycloth or velveteen, transfer the design to tissue paper or organdy and pin it onto the fabric. This prevents the stitches from getting lost in the pile.

If you wish to machine embroider a knit, use only a moderate stretch knit. Hand baste organdy or interfacing to the *wrong* side of the knit fabric beneath the design, to prevent shifting or stretching while you machine stitch.

Use an embroidery hoop with an adjustable screw to keep your fabric taut as you stitch. Insert the fabric into the hoop as shown in **Ill. 4**; it's the reverse of the way fabric is inserted for hand embroidery.

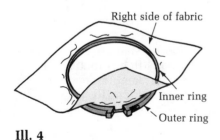

Right side of fabric

Inner ring

Outer ring

Ill. 4

Machine preparation. Remove the presser foot and ankle and lower the feed dogs. Consult your sewing machine manual for specific directions.

To make stitches that are smooth on the surface, use thread that is strong but not heavyweight for the upper thread. An extra-fine or a basting thread in the bobbin reduces fabric puckering.

Stitching. Place the hoop under the machine needle. Then *lower the presser foot lever;* though it can be hard to remember, this is a very important step. Take one stitch and bring the bobbin thread up to the surface (**Ill. 5**). Secure the thread by taking several stitches in place; then clip the thread ends. Continue stitching, following the line of your design and keeping your hands on the rim of the hoop rather than on the fabric as you direct it.

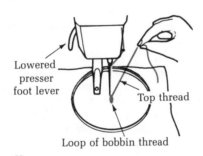

Lowered presser foot lever

Top thread

Loop of bobbin thread

Ill. 5

On the first test sample, check thread tensions. If the bobbin thread appears on the surface, loosen the upper thread tension. If that doesn't solve the problem, consult your sewing machine manual.

By setting the machine on a straight stitch, you can create line drawings similar to a pencil line, with greater flexibility than with a programmed stitch.

For satin stitch monograms or outlined designs, set the machine on a zigzag stitch. Keep one edge of the zigzag stitch along the design's lines to ensure smooth, straight edges (**Ill. 6**). Keep all stitches horizontal by moving the hoop straight toward you and away from you, working gradually from the left side of the design to the right as you would write with a pencil. Never move the hoop diagonally or rotate it.

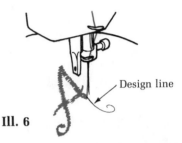

Design line

Ill. 6

To fill in embroidery designs, move the hoop rapidly back and forth horizontally to create a hand satin stitch effect. You'll be blending the stitches as if coloring with a crayon (**Ill. 7**).

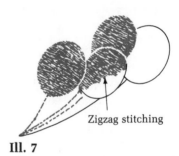

Zigzag stitching

Ill. 7

When one area of color in your design is complete, take a few stitches in place to secure the thread; clip the thread ends close to the fabric. Begin a fresh area of color as described above. When the design is done, bring the presser foot lever up and remove the hoop from the machine bed. If you used tissue paper or reinforcing fabric, cut away any that remains.

Embroidery

A trail of flower buds, a loco-motive and boxcars, hearts, ducks, or even dinosaurs can find their way onto a garment and into young hearts with the help of some embroidered stitches. Though you usually em-broider garment pieces before they're assembled, you can also embroider a completed or pur-chased garment. Many pattern transfer and embroidery design books are available at needle-work shops. Or you can create your own designs (see "How to transfer a design," page 38).

Materials & supplies

First, choose your fabric and thread. Then, with some needles and a hoop, you're ready to get your embroidery project underway.

Fabric. The fabric of most chil-dren's clothes is sturdy and firmly woven—just right for embroidery. But all kinds of fabric—even knee socks—can be embroidered.

Whatever fabric you embel-lish, preshrink it before you em-broider it. If you plan to make a counted cross stitch design on a fabric with an uneven weave, a napped fabric, or a knit, use waste canvas to guide your stitches (see "Stitchery magic," facing page).

Thread. Six-strand embroidery floss is the most common em-broidery thread. Separate it into two-strand pieces for stitching. Pearl cotton, another favorite, is available in two thicknesses, size 3 and size 5. For an accent that sparkles, try a metallic or rayon thread.

Choose your thread accord-ing to the desired effect of the design. Pearl cotton, for exam-ple, is thicker and therefore more prominent and less delicate than embroidery floss.

Needles. The needle you use must have an eye large enough to allow your choice of thread to pass through easily.

Sharps and crewels are the needles recommended for embroidery. For most stitches, a sharply pointed needle is best. Try a chenille needle if you pre-fer a particularly large eye and a sharp point for your stitching. A blunt point is necessary for counted cross stitch, to avoid piercing the fabric's threads.

Hoop. The tautness of the fabric in an embroidery hoop prevents puckered, uneven stitching. In-sert the fabric, *right* side up, across the top edge of the hoop's inner ring. As you tighten the outer ring's tension, make sure the fabric is held taut, with straight grain.

If you've already cut out a garment pattern piece and the fabric isn't large enough to fit into an embroidery hoop, baste scrap fabric pieces to its sides to increase the surface area.

Basic stitches

You can make exciting needle-work designs using only a few simple stitches. The basic in-structions below apply to all types of thread.

Cut the thread in lengths of 18 to 24 inches. Longer threads may begin to untwist or fray at the ends from being pulled through the fabric.

To embroider clothing or quilts that will receive hard wear and lots of laundering, attach the first thread to your fabric by tak-ing several tiny backstitches in an area you'll cover later with stitches. (Avoid knots—they can slip and come untied; use them only on a project that won't be worn or handled regularly, such as a sampler or wall hanging.)

To finish a thread, weave it through several stitches on the *wrong* side of the fabric; cut the thread close to the fabric's sur-face. Start new threads by weav-ing them in the same manner.

Straight stitch. For details such as facial features or flower sta-mens, use stitches in a row, radi-ating from one point, or ran-domly (**Ill. 1**).

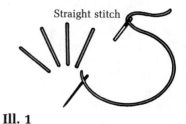

Straight stitch

Ill. 1

Running stitch. Use to designate lines. Keep stitches and spaces uniform in length (**Ill. 2**).

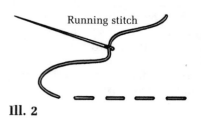

Running stitch

Ill. 2

Outline or stem stitch. Names describe stitch function. Keep thread on same side of needle with each stitch (**Ill. 3**).

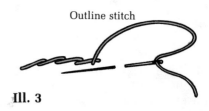

Outline stitch

Ill. 3

Satin stitch. Align stitches side by side, with no gaps, to fill in an area of color. Start in center of area to be filled and stitch to one end; return to center and continue to opposite end (**Ill. 4**).

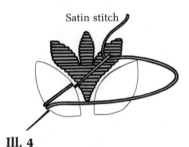

Satin stitch

Ill. 4

Backstitch. Work from right to left with uniform stitch lengths, with beginning of one stitch touching end of another. Use for outlining or lettering (**Ill. 5**).

Backstitch

Ill. 5

Cross stitch. Work a row of half cross stitches from left to right; work back, stitching the other half. Upper half-cross of all stitches must slant in same direction to prevent a haphazard shading effect (**Ill. 6**). *Counted cross stitch* is worked on even-weave fabric, using a graph as a reference for stitch placement.

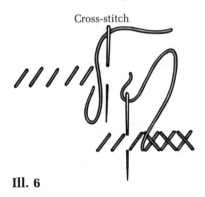

Cross-stitch

Ill. 6

Blanket stitch. This makes a good border. Hold thread loop until needle and thread are pulled through fabric so that each stitch secures previous loop (**Ill. 7**).

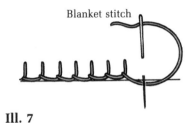

Blanket stitch

Ill. 7

Chain stitch. Hold thread loop until needle reemerges. Anchor last chain by inserting needle on other side of loop (**Ill. 8**).

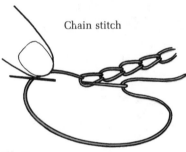

Chain stitch

Ill. 8

French knot. This stitch adds dimension to designs. Twist thread clockwise around needle; hold thread taut as needle is pulled through fabric (**Ill. 9**). To make a *bullion stitch*, continue twisting the thread 5 or 6 times around the needle.

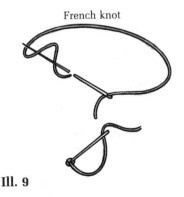

French knot

Ill. 9

Stitchery magic

You have just the perfect counted cross stitch pattern to decorate a baby's socks or a boy's denims, a turtleneck, T-shirt, or terrycloth robe. But how can you cross stitch on fabric with an uneven weave? Your problem is solved: now there's a starched cotton canvas called *waste canvas*. Use it as directed below to provide an even-weave surface wherever necessary.

Baste a piece of waste canvas on the fabric's right side, over the area to be cross stitched. Use a blunt needle for loose-weave fabrics and a sharp one for dense fabrics such as denim. Stab stitch your cross stitch design through both layers, using the even weave canvas as a guide for your pattern. A hoop isn't necessary, since the canvas is stiff enough to provide a firm surface.

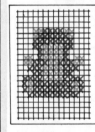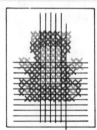

When the pattern is complete, pull out the basting threads and dampen the canvas to remove the sizing (on satin or velvet, use only steam). Carefully pull the canvas threads, one by one, out of the stitching. Pull all the vertical ones first, then all the horizontal ones. Tweezers make the job easier. The cross stitching remains on the surface of the fabric.

Waste canvas is available in many sizes, and is purchased by the yard.

Smocking sweethearts

A classic decorative treatment, smocking never goes out of style. Its attractive stitches and soft gathers transform the plainest of garments into a delight to behold. Smocking gathers in fullness at a yoke, a bodice, or cuffs; a smocked panel insert livens up a garment. Both techniques add splendor to boys' and girls' clothing.

Smocking

Does the sight of a little smocked garment make you sigh in memory of your own childhood favorite? The timeless craft of smocking—working embroidery stitches over gathers of fabric—is still popular today, transforming the simplest garments into heirloom treasures.

Don't let the complicated look of smocking deceive you. Once you've mastered a few basic stitches, it's surprisingly simple to make beautiful patterns.

There are two distinct methods of smocking: American and English. In American smocking, you gather the pleats as you work the decorative stitches. English smocking has two separate steps: you gather the fabric first, then work decorative stitches over the gathers. The English technique, described below, ensures more consistent results.

You can work English smocking into a garment in two ways. In its traditional role, smocking gathers in the fullness of the fabric at such spots as sleeves, waist, and yoke. But it can also be a smocked panel, inserted into a garment for a purely decorative effect.

Materials & supplies

Whether you plan to use smocking as an integral part of the garment or as a decorative insert, complete the smocking before constructing the garment. Since the garment is likely to be a special outfit, use the best materials possible to ensure long-lasting results.

Fabric. Use light to medium-weight fabrics for smocked garments. Natural fibers are recommended since they hold the shape of pleats well; synthetics are difficult to shape.

If you're inexperienced with smocking, it's best to begin with a garment pattern designed for smocking. If you choose an unsmocked pattern, cut the fabric pieces for the area to be smocked 2½ to 3 times as wide as the desired finished width of the area. The amount you increase depends on the fabric you use; heavier fabrics should have less fullness.

Thread & needle. Six-strand embroidery floss and pearl cotton are used for smocking stitches. The embroidery floss—separated into three-strand pieces—provides a delicate look on lightweight fabrics, and is especially good for intricate, close stitches. Use additional strands with heavier fabrics. Size 5 pearl cotton is bolder and more durable, suitable for heavy fabrics and playclothes. It works well with open patterns of stitches.

An embroidery (crewel) needle works best for smocking.

Pleating

The fabric area to be smocked must first be gathered into many pleats. You can save much time and effort by pleating with a gathering machine. Though the machine is expensive, many fabric and needlework stores have them and offer a pleating service; try to find a store that does. Otherwise, mark and gather the fabric by hand.

Marking the fabric. Evenly spaced dots are used to mark the placement of gathering stitches and to determine the width of the fabric pleats. Iron-on transfer dots are available in various sizes (also referred to as gauges)—use a size with wider dot spacing for heavier fabrics. Or

draw your own dots with a transfer pencil.

Before you begin marking the fabric, make sure the grainline is straight. Working on the fabric's *wrong* side, position dots parallel with the grainline, covering the entire area to be smocked. To draw your own dots, space them from edge to edge, ⅛ inch to ⅜ inch apart both vertically and horizontally (farther apart on heavier fabrics).

Gathering the fabric. For the gathering thread, use a double strand of regular sewing thread, or a single strand of button and carpet thread, in a color that contrasts with the fabric and smocking threads (it will be removed later). Run the thread through beeswax to help prevent knotting and breaking.

Work from right to left on the *wrong* side of the fabric, using a new thread for each row. Complete each row with one continuous thread.

Start each row by knotting the thread end and taking a stitch in place at the farthest right-hand dot. Take running stitches across the entire area to be smocked, picking up a dot per stitch (**Ill. 1**). It will be easier to take the stitches if you roll the fabric over the ' index finger of the hand holding the fabric.

Pick up dot with each running stitch

Ill. 1

Let the thread end hang down from the end of each row. When all the rows are stitched,

pull the gathering threads to form tight pleats in the fabric. Gather the fabric until it's about 1 inch narrower than the desired finished width, to allow for slight expansion when the gathering threads are removed.

Holding the fabric at the top and bottom edges, snap it firmly to make the pleats fall into place. Use an iron to steam the pleats; don't press.

Tie the ends of adjacent gathering threads together to keep them from pulling out while you're smocking. The gathering threads will serve as guidelines for the smocking stitches.

Designing stitch patterns

You can purchase garment patterns that include smocking designs, or buy separate smocking designs known as plates. Or you can design your own pattern of stitches. Carefully plan the use of color and stitch types so the pattern maintains vertical balance—with the rows neither too close together nor too far apart.

The elasticity of the smocking is an important consideration if your smocking is controlling the garment's fullness. Certain stitches—such as the wave and the trellis—are elastic and allow the fabric to stretch. Others—such as the cable and the outline—have very little give and hold the fabric firmly. Choose a balanced combination of elastic and controlled stitches to get the best performance from your smocking. If too many elastic stitches are used, the smocking will be limp. With too much control, the smocking won't have elasticity. Use controlled stitches where the most control is needed: at neckline and cuff edges, for example.

(Continued on page 30)

Basic stitches

Though there are many different smocking stitches, they all stem from a few basic stitches that are easy to learn. Just space, repeat, or combine these basic stitches for unlimited variations.

As you work each stitch across the fabric, refer to these pointers for the best results.

● Stitches are worked from left to right, using the gathering threads as guidelines to keep the smocking straight and evenly spaced.

● Start each row with a knot on the *wrong* side of the fabric; take one stitch in place at the first pleat on the left. To finish a row, bring the thread back to the *wrong* side of the fabric after the stitch at the last pleat to the right. Secure the thread with a knot; cut the thread end.

● Hold the needle horizontally as you work; pick up only the top third of a pleat with each stitch. If you pick up more fabric, you'll decrease the elasticity of the smocking.

● Work with an even tension, pulling each stitch so it's snug, but not too tight.

● If a new thread is needed in the middle of a row, bring the working thread to the *wrong* side of the fabric between two pleats. Secure it with a knot and cut it. Start the new thread at the same place by knotting it and bringing it up in the space where you want the stitch to continue.

Outline and stem stitch. These stitches are identical except for the direction they slant. Because rows of outline and stem stitches have little stretch, they're often used to control gathers at the top and bottom of the smocked area.

To make a row of outline stitches, start the thread at the first pleat on the left. Take a stitch from right to left through the second pleat, keeping the thread *above* the needle; pull the stitch snugly. Repeat the stitch in the next pleat, keeping the thread above the needle and stitching parallel to the gathering-thread line (**Ill. 2**). Finish with the last stitch in the last pleat to the right.

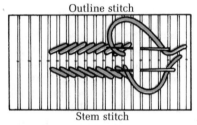

Outline stitch

Stem stitch

Ill. 2

The stem stitch is worked the same way, except that you keep the thread *below* the needle as you make each stitch.

Cable stitch. This stitch is quite inelastic; use it as you would the outline stitch, to control gathers. Use it also for *back-smocking* in areas where no stitches appear on the right side. Worked on the *wrong* side of the fabric, back-smocking prevents the pleats from puffing out of shape.

Work this stitch as you would the outline stitch, but alternate the position of the thread: above the needle for one stitch, below the needle for the next (**Ill. 3**).

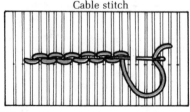

Cable stitch

Ill. 3

Wave or chevron stitch. A variation of the cable stitch, the wave stitch is very elastic and exercises little fabric control.

Begin at the first pleat on the left, at a gathering-thread line. Make sure there's another gathering-thread line above the one you're using as a guide. Work a cable stitch with the thread below the needle. Move up half a row and, inserting the needle in the right-hand side, pick up the next pleat, keeping the thread below the needle; pull it snug. Complete a cable stitch by picking up the fourth pleat, keeping the thread above the needle.

Move down to the gathering-thread line and pick up the next free pleat, inserting the needle from the right and keeping the thread above the needle. Repeat the above procedure to the right-hand end of the pleats (**Ill. 4**).

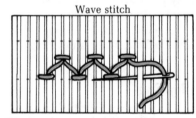

Wave stitch

Ill. 4

Surface honeycomb stitch. Another cable stitch variation, the surface honeycomb stitch has little control, permitting a lot of elasticity in the smocking.

With the thread below the needle, make a cable stitch in the first two pleats along the gathering-thread line. Move up half a row and take the next stitch as you would for the wave stitch (above), but pick up the *second* and *third*, rather than the third and fourth, pleats in the cable stitch. Continue as for the wave stitch, but overlap each upper and lower cable stitch one pleat instead of proceeding to the next free pleat. Repeat the procedure to the end of the pleats (**Ill. 5**).

Surface honeycomb stitch

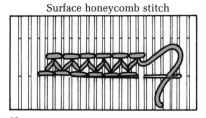

Ill. 5

Trellis stitch. This is an elastic stitch with a lot of stretch. It's versatile: layer it to make chevrons; invert alternate rows to make diamonds. The stitch begins at one gathering-thread line, works diagonally up to the next gathering-thread line, turns, and works back down.

Start at the first pleat on the left with a stem stitch. Then work four stem stitches, each one moving up one quarter of the space between the gathering threads. Make an outline stitch along the upper gathering thread. Then work down with four outline stitches. Repeat the procedure across the fabric (**Ill. 6**).

Trellis stitch

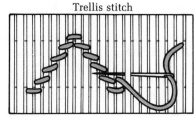

Ill. 6

Finishing

Carefully remove the gathering threads and shape the smocking to its finished size. With an iron, steam it to set the pleats (don't press or you'll flatten the smocking). Continue with the garment construction as your pattern directs.

Hearts aplenty

Use a clever combination of simple stitches and—voila!—rows of smocked hearts adorn a special garment. This smocking is designed to fit into a garment as a decorative insert. Repeat the 3½-inch-high design to fit the width you need.

Cut lightweight fabric to the desired height plus 2 seam allowances; cut it three times as wide as the desired finished width, plus two seam allowances. Use three strands of embroidery floss in each of three different colors for decorative stitches. Use directions under "Smocking," beginning on page 28. Mark pleating dots ¼ inch apart, spacing rows ½ inch apart. Gather and secure the pleats.

● First gathering-thread line: Using color A, cable stitch.

● Second line: Using color B, wave stitch, extending stitch halfway down to next gathering-thread line.

● Third line: Using color B, alternate trellis stitch and wave stitch. Exaggerate each trellis so that it extends from bottom of wave stitch at second gathering-thread line to ¾ the depth between lines 3 and 4. Needle should enter pleat at a 45° angle with each stitch in the trellis. Wave stitch should extend halfway down to next gathering-thread line.

● Fourth line: Using color C, trellis stitch with needle at 45° angle for each stitch. Start at bottom of wave stitch in third gathering-thread line; end halfway between lines 4 and 5.

Repeat the above rows of stitches in reverse order to create a mirror image.

Design: Nan Turner.

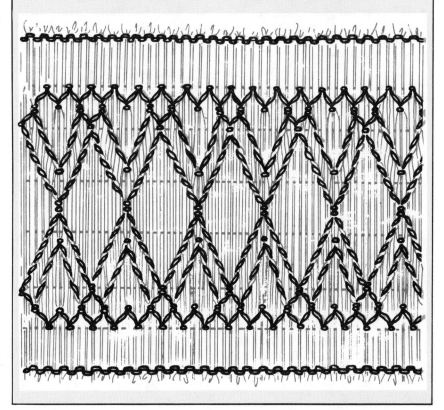

Tapes & trims

Piping, braid, and bias tape can add bursts of color to any youngster's outfit. Laces, ribbons, and ruching give a garment a feminine aura that little girls love. Combined tapes and trims can create sensational garments for both girls and boys, from infants to preschoolers—and beyond.

Cutting bias strips

Strips of fabric, cut on the bias, are a staple item used in making such trims as bias tape (see below) and piping (see page 34). They can also form the basis of other decorative elements, such as ruffles (see page 15). Below are two methods of cutting fabric for bias strips.

In the first method, used primarily to cut strips for short lengths of trim, straighten the fabric and trim it evenly along the crosswise grain. Then fold the fabric so the selvage is aligned with the crosswise grain (**Ill. 1**).

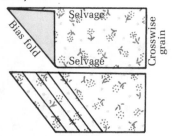

Ill. 1

Press or mark along the bias fold. Open the fabric and measure, mark, and cut bias strips of the appropriate width, using the bias foldline as your guideline.

Continuous bias strips. For projects requiring extensive lengths of bias tape, this method is the fastest and most efficient. For example, ½ yard of 45-inch-wide fabric yields about 12 continuous yards of 1½-inch-wide bias strip.

Fold a fabric square diagonally and cut along the crease line (**Ill. 2**). Positioning triangles as shown, stitch a ¼-inch seam; press the seam open. Use a diagonal edge as a guideline to measure and mark strips of the correct width, parallel to the edge.

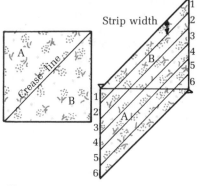

Ill. 2

With edges mismatched as shown, stitch edges together in a ¼-inch seam, forming a tube (**Ill. 3**). Cut along marked lines to form a spiral strip.

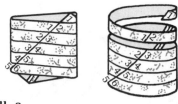

Ill. 3

Bias tape

Bias tape is a wonderfully useful and versatile trim. It's the perfect finish for either straight or curved fabric edges because of its stretch and flexibility.

Use bias tape on garments you make yourself to replace facings, encase raw edges, or make garments reversible (see "Taped seam" on page 16). You can also use it as an accent trim at pocket or hem edges on ready-made clothes or ones you make yourself.

Make your own bias tape from your garment fabric or contrasting fabrics, using the directions that follow. Or use prepackaged tapes. Several widths and styles are available, the most common being ½-inch-wide single-fold bias tape. Its edges are folded under to meet at the middle.

Double-fold bias tape goes one step further than the single fold tape: it has an extra fold slightly off the center line. This extra fold makes the tape ready to use to encase raw edges.

Making bias tape. Make your own bias tape any width you desire, depending on the degree of boldness you want. Use your garment fabric if it's light to medium weight, or use light to medium-weight cotton or cotton/polyester blend. Avoid loosely woven or crease-resistant fabrics that won't hold a press.

Though ½ inch is the most common finished width for bias tape, wrap a piece of scrap fabric over the edge of the garment to be trimmed, to decide if you need more or less width. To determine the necessary length, measure from edge to edge all the garment seams that will require bias tape; add 1 inch per seam for seam allowances. Choose the appropriate cutting method from "Cutting bias strips," above. Cut the bias strips the desired width plus ½ inch.

Fold the raw edges of the bias tape under ¼ inch, *wrong* sides together; press. This step will be much less time consuming if you use a bias tape maker; it will automatically fold the edges.

If you wish to make your single-fold tape into double-fold

tape, fold it in half lengthwise, *wrong* sides together, and press. Make the fold slightly off-center, so one side of the tape is approximately ¹⁄₁₆ inch wider than the other.

If the bias tape will be used on a curved surface, steam it to fit the curve before applying it to the garment.

Encasing a raw edge. You can apply bias tape to a raw edge in one of two ways. A combination of hand and machine stitching gives a polished look; machine stitching alone provides a quick, sporty, topstitched finish.

To encase an edge with a combination of hand and machine stitching, begin by trimming the garment seam allowances to a width slightly narrower than the finished bias tape. On an edge that was originally designed to be sewn into a seam, such as an armhole or neckline, you'll need to cut away the entire garment seam allowance before applying bias tape.

Cut the tape to the length of the edge to be covered, plus 1 inch. When the tape will make a continuous band around the opening, such as at an armhole or a hem edge, fold one narrow end of the tape under ½ inch; pin in place in an inconspicuous area. The unfolded end of the tape should overlap the folded end ½ inch (**Ill. 4**).

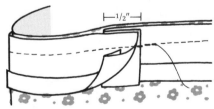

Ill. 4

If the garment edge has an opening or is part of a separate piece, such as a neckline or a
(Continued on page 34)

The winning edge

Bias tape along the edge of a hem, armhole, or neckline can bring a garment to life, and a surprise touch of piping in a seam or along an edge makes any garment an instant success. Use contrasting colors or prints for dramatic emphasis. Try a metallic piping for a little dazzle, satin piping in velour garments for sheen, or velveteen in wool for softness.

Glow in the dark

All parents worry that their children won't be visible when playing outside. Adding reflective tape to outdoor clothing and gear can help lessen these worries. Two types of reflective tape—reflective and fluorescent—are available in fabric strips or patches. (Bicycle stores are the most likely place to find both these products.)

Reflective material is made up of tiny beads that reflect light beams, such as those from headlights of approaching cars, back to their source. It's more effective than fluorescent material at night, but it doesn't glow in daylight.

Fluorescent material both emits and reflects light, so it seems to glow on its own. It's more effective in the daytime than at night.

Apply these tapes to anything your child might wear or carry in the evening. Don't forget umbrellas, boots, and Halloween costumes. Several colors are available; you can choose one that coordinates with the garment's colors.

Use strips of tape to make stripes or chevrons on sleeves and pants, or rows around a hem. Cut patches into shapes and add them like appliqués for a whimsical touch. How about reflective tape clouds on a vinyl slicker or a row of stars around the hem of a parka?

patch pocket, turn both narrow ends under ½ inch to create a finished edge.

After pinning the tape to the garment, stitch along the tape foldline; clip any curves.

Fold the tape over to encase the seam. On the wrong side of the garment, pin the long folded edge of the tape to the garment near the stitching line, and slipstitch by hand (**Ill. 5**). These stitches shouldn't show on the front of the garment. Slipstitch the ends closed.

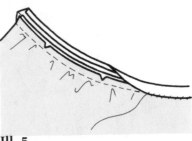

Ill. 5

For the topstitched application, use double-fold bias tape, cutting it and the garment edge as described above. With the wider side of the tape on the inside of the garment, slip the folded tape over the raw edge to encase it. Fold and overlap the ends of the tape as described above; pin the tape in place. Machine stitch close to the free edge of the tape, taking care to catch both the outside and the inside layers of the tape. Slipstitch the ends closed.

Piping

Piping— fabric-covered cord— is a purely decorative trim, but— wow!—can it make a difference in a garment's appearance! You can use it to define seam lines, accent unusual features, provide a special edge finish, or add a spark of color to any garment you make yourself.

Finished piping is available in fabric stores, but you can make your own in any size or color. Use light to medium-weight fabrics to cover the cord; try satin, metallic, or velveteen fabrics for dynamic effects.

Cable cord is used as the filler in piping. The ⅛-inch width is usually recommended for children's wear, but use a thicker cord for heavy fabrics or a special effect.

Making piping. Measure from edge to edge the length of each seam where you plan to add piping. Use this measurement to determine the lengths of bias fabric and cord you'll need. Cut bias strips, using the appropriate method under "Cutting bias strips" on page 32. Make the strips wide enough to fit comfortably around your choice of cord, adding two ½-inch seam allowances.

Wrap a strip, *right* side out, around a cord, keeping the raw edges even. Using a zipper foot, baste close to the cord without crowding it; later, you'll stitch the garment seam between the basting and the cord.

Piping a seam. Pin the piping to the *right* side of one of the garment pieces along the seamline, with the cording extending over the seamline on the inside, matching the piping stitching line to the garment seamline. If the seam curves, clip the piping seam allowance as needed (**Ill. 6**).

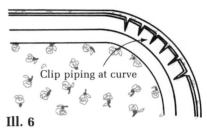

Clip piping at curve

Ill. 6

At an outside corner, clip the piping seam allowance to allow it to make a 90-degree turn (**Ill. 7**).

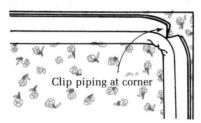
Clip piping at corner

Ill. 7

Using a zipper foot, baste the piping to the garment, stitching on the piping stitching line.

Pin the garment pieces, *right* sides together, with the piped garment piece on top. Using a zipper foot, sew the seam, stitching slightly to the garment side of the visible row of basting.

Piping an edge. When piping an edge, such as that of a vest or sleeve cuff, you must start and finish the piping in an inconspicuous spot, such as under the arm or at the shoulder seam. Make the piping 1½ inches longer than the length needed (see "Making piping" for the method of calculating dimensions). Pull the cord out of the piping fabric and snip off ¾ inch from each end. Install the piping in the seam between the garment and its facing, using the directions in "Piping a seam" (see facing page) for basting and sewing. Overlap the empty ends of the piping, as shown, curving the piping ends down below the seamline for a smooth, finished edge (**Ill. 8**).

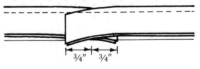
¾" ¾"

Ill. 8

Covered cording. Covered cording is similar to piping, but the seam is finished; the seam allowances aren't visible. Your pattern may call for it for making button loops, straps, and various trims that aren't stitched into a seamline.

To make cording, cut a length of ⅛-inch cord twice the desired finished length suggested by your pattern. Using the directions under "Cutting bias strips" on page 32, cut a bias strip of fabric the desired finished length plus ½ inch. Make the strip wide enough to fit around the cord, adding two ½-inch seam allowances.

Starting at one end of the cord, wrap the bias strip around the cord with the *wrong* side of the fabric facing out and the raw edges even. The fabric will cover only half the length of the cord.

Using a zipper foot, stitch along the length of the fabric, close to the cording. Stitch from the end of the cord that is enclosed in fabric to the other end of the fabric. Then stitch across the end of the fabric, through the cord, leaving the same seam allowance as you did along the lengthwise seam. Trim the lengthwise seam close to the stitching (**Ill. 9**)

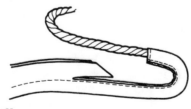

Ill. 9

Turn the fabric right side out, pulling it over the uncovered end of the cord. Cut off the newly exposed end of the cord as close as possible to the fabric end. Install the cording as your pattern directs.

Ruching

Have you ever heard of ruching? Borrowed from Victorian dress, ruching is a pretty way to turn a garment into a treasure. It can liven up a ready-made garment or be the crowning touch on one you make yourself.

Ruching is a pleated strip of fabric, stitched to a garment's surface. Use a single row of ruching to outline a neck edge or front placket, or to echo the line of a hem. Add vertical rows to create frills on the front of a bodice or christening gown.

Preparing the fabric. Use a light to medium-weight fabric for ruching, or substitute ½-inch-wide ribbon or galloon lace (a lace finished decoratively along both sides).

If you're using fabric, cut it into 2½-inch-wide bias strips, using the directions in "Cutting bias strips" on page 32. Whether you're using fabric, ribbon, or lace, make the length of the strip 2½ times the desired finished length, measuring the pattern pieces to determine the finished length needed.

If the strip is fabric, fold it in half lengthwise, *right* sides together; add thread, following the instructions below for ease in reversing a fabric tube. Pin the strip's sides together. Stitch along the length of the strip, ¼ inch from the raw edge. Press the seam open and turn the fabric tube *right* side out to make the ruching strip. Press the ruching strip so the seam lies down the middle of the back. (Ribbon and lace are already the appropriate width and require no preparatory folding or stitching.)

NOTE: To facilitate turning long tubes of fabric inside out, place a piece of heavy thread or
(Continued on page 36)

narrow cording inside the fabric near the fold before stitching the tube. Let the thread extend out both ends. Stitch it to one end of the fabric, to secure it; then stitch the fabric tube's seam without letting the thread get caught in it.

Pull the free end of the thread, which in turn will pull the fabric tube *right* side out. Cut the thread from the fabric.

Making box pleat ruching. Mark the ruching strip alternately at ½-inch and ¼-inch intervals. Form pleats by folding along the markings, alternately folding toward the right and left as shown (**Ill. 10**). The upper and lower pleats will be ½ inch wide. Pin the pleats as you fold them. Baste down the center of the ruching strip.

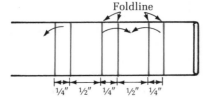

Ill. 10

Mark a line on the garment to use as a ruching placement guideline. Starting at a side seam, pin the ruching to the *right* side of the garment. Stitch down the center of the ruching strip to attach the ruching to the garment; remove basting (**Ill. 11**).

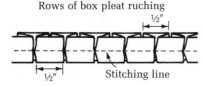

Rows of box pleat ruching

Stitching line

Ill. 11

Making rose ruching. Make the box pleat ruching described above and attach it to the garment. Gather the center of each upper pleat by whipstitching it

in the center with a double strand of thread, anchoring each whipstitch at the stitching line (**Ill. 12**).

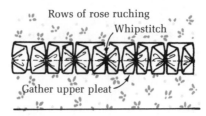

Rows of rose ruching
Whipstitch
Gather upper pleat

Ill. 12

Ribbons for trim

There are ribbons to suit all situations. Take a trip to the fabric store to contemplate all the possibilities. Some ribbons are soft velvet; some have pretty filigree work on the sides. Dots, stripes, delicate flowers, or lines of trains, whales, or boats ornament the surface of satin and grosgrain ribbons. Deciding where to put such ribbons is fun—don't be afraid to mix and match. Use them to touch up a hand-me-down or to add a spark of color to a garment you make yourself.

Ribbon is available either packaged or by the yard. Check to be sure the fiber content is compatible with your garment. Pretreat ribbons as you would your fabric; most are preshrunk and washable.

Simplify sewing by securing the ribbon to the fabric with a fabric glue stick. If the ribbon ends won't be sewn into a seam, turn the raw edges under to prevent raveling.

Attach ⅛-inch-wide ribbon by stitching down the middle. For wider ribbon, edgestitch along each side (**Ill. 13**). Try attaching solid colored ribbon with programmed stitching for an interesting effect.

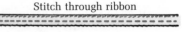

Stitch through ribbon

Ill. 13

You can hand sew ribbon in place, using embroidery floss; incorporate a variety of embroidery stitches (**Ill. 14**).

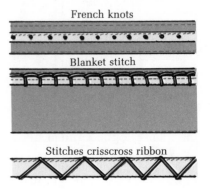

French knots

Blanket stitch

Stitches crisscross ribbon

Ill. 14

A touch of lace

Lace is a bit of detail that never goes out of style. Just a touch of lace at a collar or cuff alters the look of any garment you've made or bought. Add more, and you'll transform a simple garment into a treasured party dress.

Lace is available in a number of different fiber contents. For children's clothes, washability is a must. Remember to preshrink lace before using it.

Gathered lace. Some laces are available preruffled, or you can gather lace into ruffles yourself (follow the directions on page 15, making only one row of gathering stitches close to the lace's edge). The seams of collars, cuffs, and yokes beg to be embellished with ruffled lace trim. Stitch it into the seams like piping (see page 34).

Flat lace. Many types of flat lace are available. Single-edged lace, such as eyelet, is used in the same manner as gathered lace. It's also used like piping along garment edges. Double-edged flat lace—for example, the type called *beading*, with slits through which you can weave ribbon—is sewn directly to a fabric surface, not into a seam. For a particularly delicate, airy application, try the insertion method below, adding the lace before the garment is completed.

Lace insertion. Pin flat lace in place on the *right* side of the garment piece; zigzag stitch along each edge, using thread the color of the garment fabric. Turn the garment to the *wrong* side and cut the fabric lengthwise behind the lace, midway between the stitched lines. Trim the fabric to within ¼ inch of each stitched edge and hand sew a rolled hem on each side (**Ill. 15**).

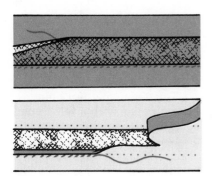

Ill. 15

Places for laces, ribbons & bows

Use ribbons and lace to decorate all kinds of garments, from playwear to fancy dresses. Line them up row after row for a new yoke look; let them peek out of unexpected places. Trim pockets or cuffs, cover seams, or highlight fabric inserts. Add a surprise touch of lacy color to a dark outfit, or a line of ducks on a ribbon to the bib of coveralls.

How to transfer a design

Delight a child by adding a personalized touch to clothing, toys, or any fabric project with designs appliquéd, embroidered, or even painted onto fabric.

Before you begin to sew, stitch, or paint, you have to get the pattern onto your fabric. Below you'll find several methods for enlarging or reducing patterns to the size you need, and for transferring that pattern to your fabric.

Reducing & enlarging a pattern

You've found the perfect elephant shape to appliqué onto a pair of jeans, but it's in a book and it's not quite the right size. What do you do? Use one of the techniques below to enlarge or reduce the design.

Photocopying. For fast, accurate results, take your pattern to a photocopy service. For a small fee, you can have the pattern enlarged or reduced on paper or transparent vellum. Better quality reproductions are available at a higher cost, and some photocopy services can reproduce in color.

Overhead projector. To resize a number of patterns, overhead projectors are available for rent at audio-visual equipment stores. A projector is the best solution when you want to make a substantial enlargement.

Making a grid. You can use a grid to size a pattern without mechanical aids. To do so, you'll need a supply of vellum graph paper.

Place the graph paper over the pattern and trace the design. Identify each vertical and horizontal row with numbers and letters. Determine by measuring the design how much it must be enlarged or reduced to become the proper size. Then choose a grid that much larger or smaller than the original grid. For example, if you've traced a design onto graph paper with ¼-inch grid squares and the design must double in size, choose a grid with ½-inch squares.

To make the new grid, either use another graph paper or draw your own grid, scaled to the proper size. Mark the new grid with the same numbering system you used for the original grid. Transfer the pattern lines carefully from grid box to equivalent grid box (see below).

Original design

Enlarged design

Transferring a pattern

Now you're ready to transfer your design to your fabric, using one of the transfer methods below. Preshrink and press your fabric before transferring a pattern to it.

Light table. Most of us don't have access to an electric light table, but on a sunny day, it's easy to create your own. Light to medium-weight fabrics that are light in color are easiest to work with.

Trace your pattern onto tracing paper. Tape the paper, *right* side up, onto a window. Center your fabric, *right* side up, over the paper and tape it in place. Trace the pattern outlines onto the fabric (see "Other marking tools," below).

Dressmaker's carbon. Washable dressmaker's carbon paper is ideal for use on most fabrics, except those with a nap.

Tape your fabric, *right* side up, to a hard, flat surface. Center and pin the pattern to the fabric, leaving the bottom edge free. Slip the carbon paper, shiny side down, between the fabric and the pattern.

With an empty ballpoint pen or blunt pencil, trace the pattern outlines. Press firmly but carefully to avoid tearing the pattern paper.

Heat-transfer pencil. Use this method for smooth-textured fabrics from light to heavy in weight. You'll find transfer pencils in fabric stores.

Trace your pattern onto tracing paper with a felt-tipped pen. Flip the tracing paper to the *wrong* side and retrace the design lines with the transfer pencil.

Center and pin the paper, *right* side up, to the *right* side of the fabric so the transfer pencil marks are against the fabric. Press the paper-and-fabric sandwich according to the pencil manufacturer's instructions.

Other marking tools. Use dressmaker's chalk or a pencil to mark pattern symbols and placement lines onto your fabric.

Appliqué

Add an appliqué to a garment and watch the owner's smile grow! Playful and practical, appliqués are always a welcome addition.

Appliqué consists of shapes cut from one piece of fabric and applied to another. Use appliqués to add color and pattern, hide a stain or tear, or even name names. The shapes, sizes, and colors you choose make an appliquéd garment a personalized possession.

Traditionally, appliqué is stitched by hand, but the zigzag stitch on your sewing machine permits a contemporary version of the art. Machine appliqué is recommended for most children's clothes and toys because it's a faster and more durable technique than hand stitching.

Appliqué techniques are the same whether you're in the process of making a garment or are enhancing a completed one. Below are the techniques of fabric preparation and stitching that will help you achieve the most pleasing results.

Getting ready

Before you begin stitching your appliqué, make a few preparations: consider the suitability of the garment you want to appliqué, choose fabric and thread, make a pattern, and cut out the fabric pieces.

Which garment? You can add an appliqué to a garment made of just about any fabric, from lightweight cotton to velveteen.

As long as you don't use a very detailed or large pattern, you can machine appliqué even on a knit fabric. To prevent the knit from stretching, hand baste a nonwoven, nonfusible interfacing to the *wrong* side of the fabric, underlying the area you plan to appliqué. Stitch the appliqué through both the fabric and the interfacing. When the appliqué has been stitched, cut the interfacing away as close to the stitching as possible.

Appliqué fabric. You can use just about any fabric for an appliqué; it needn't be the same type of fabric as the garment it will adorn. Tightly woven plain-weave fabrics are always good choices for appliqué, but also consider corduroy, satin, or velveteen for tactile and visual pizzazz. When you combine different fabrics, make sure they have similar care requirements.

If you're going to machine appliqué a design made of lightweight or knit fabric, add stability to the appliqué fabric by applying fusible interfacing to the *wrong* side of it *before* cutting the appliqué pieces; fuse it according to the manufacturer's directions.

Thread. Whether stitching by hand or machine, use a thread color the same as or slightly darker than the appliqué fabric color. Use a contrasting color only for dramatic effect.

Regular sewing thread is suited to both hand and machine stitching. Size 5 pearl cotton or three strands of six-strand embroidery floss add a bold, decorative look when hand-worked in an embroidery stitch.

Pattern. Your design may be as small as a flower on a collar or as large as a landscape across the back of a jacket. Whatever the size, a pattern is important for the cutting and placement of the appliqué fabric.

Begin by enlarging or reducing your appliqué design until it is the size it will be on the garment (see "Reducing and enlarging a pattern" on the facing page). If your design contains a lot of pieces, consider making two patterns: one to cut into individual pattern pieces, and one to keep as a master to guide you in placing the pieces on the garment.

Cut the pattern into separate pattern pieces, one for each separate piece of appliqué fabric. Lay these pieces on the *right* side of the appliqué fabric for machine appliqué, or on the *wrong* side for hand appliqué. Make sure the fabric grainline runs the same direction on all of the pieces. Trace each pattern piece on the fabric.

If an appliqué piece will be overlapped by another piece, extend the side that will be hidden about ½ inch beyond the pattern piece's edge to eliminate any chance that a gap will appear between appliqué pieces when you sew them down.

If you plan to machine appliqué, cut along the traced lines of each appliqué piece. If you plan to hand appliqué, add ¼ inch for the seam allowance around the perimeter of each appliqué piece before cutting.

Basting

Baste your appliqué pieces in place—using thread, glue stick, or fusible web—before stitching them, to prevent puckering and slipping.

Before you start basting, decide on the sequence in which you will add the pieces. Think of the pattern three-dimensionally; work from background to foreground. For example, to make up a scene, you would lay down first the sky, then the mountains, and finally the trees. You would lay down an ice cream cone before the ice cream.

(Continued on page 40)

Vested interests

One basic vest pattern can satisfy a child's fascination for anything from sailboats to teddy bears. Transform each vest you make with a different decorative technique. Embroidery, appliqué, or fabric paint, alone or combined, can add a colorful and whimsical touch. Add rickrack, buttons, or ribbons to personalize a vest, or enhance it with quilting to add texture.

Once you've decided on your sequence, baste and stitch each piece in the appropriate order.

Thread baste, glue, or fuse the appliqué fabric to the garment, using one of the techniques below. If you are going to appliqué by hand, keep the basting ½ inch or more from the fabric edge so that you can still turn the seam allowance under before stitching.

Thread basting. Hand baste the appliqué to the garment by taking long running stitches through both layers of fabric, using cotton basting or sewing thread. Don't stitch too close to the edge of the appliqué or the basting stitches will get caught in the appliqué stitches.

Fabric glue stick. This is handy for basting, especially to hold down corners and points. Once you've glued your appliqué in place, you can easily lift and reposition it, if necessary. The glue dissolves in the wash, leaving no stain or stiffness.

Fusible web. Cut a piece of fusible web the same size and shape as each appliqué piece. Fuse the appliqué to the garment fabric, following the manufacturer's directions.

Machine stitching

Any zigzag sewing machine can create a satin stitch to use when appliquéing. A satin stitch is a zigzag stitch with the stitches so close together that they appear to form a thick, solid line—very attractive as it outlines each appliqué piece. A bit of practice is required before you can stitch smooth lines, but once you feel confident, you'll be surprised at how quickly you can finish your appliqué project.

The first step. Slightly loosen the upper thread tension on your machine until you can see the upper thread on the underside of the fabric when you stitch a sample scrap. The bobbin thread will always be out of sight, so don't bother to change the bobbin thread when you change the upper thread color to match a new piece of appliqué fabric.

The width of the stitching depends on the weight of the appliqué fabric and the overall size of the appliqué. The more lightweight, small, or delicate the design, the narrower the satin stitch should be.

Stitching. Take a few stitches in place before starting to satin stitch. Then, for the greatest durability, stitch so that the outer edge of the satin stitch falls just outside the outer edge of the appliqué piece.

Work slowly at first to prevent thread build-up or open spaces in your stitching. Always keep the stitches perpendicular to the edge of the appliqué piece.

If your garment fabric puckers or shifts when you begin stitching, try pinning a patch of tear-away stabilizing fabric, slightly larger than your whole appliqué design, underneath your garment fabric. Stitch through the stabilizing fabric; tear away from the stitching line when the appliqué is completed.

Cornering. Try a few practice maneuvers and you'll have corners under control. Stitch all the way down one side to the very corner of the appliqué and leave the needle in the fabric on the outside swing of the zigzag stitch (**Ill. 1**). Pivot the fabric and continue stitching down the other side. Pull the fabric slightly from behind to keep it from getting

stuck and to prevent the stitches from piling on top of each other.

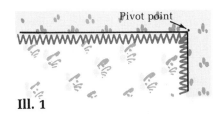

Ill. 1

Curves. Curved edges present the same problem as corners; pivoting is essential to success. When you reach a curve, insert the needle into the fabric on the curve's outside edge—into the appliqué fabric if the curve is concave; into the background fabric if the curve is convex—and pivot slightly (**Ill. 2**).

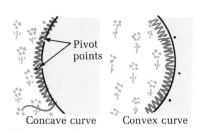

Concave curve   Convex curve

Ill. 2

Once you pivot, your next few stitches will overlap the previous stitches; pull the fabric slightly from behind to keep the stitches from piling up. Continue pivoting as necessary to work smoothly around the curve.

Points. As you approach a point while stitching, tailor the stitching to the point's configuration by gradually reducing the width of the zigzag stitch (**Ill. 3**). At the very point, insert the needle on the outside edge of the appliqué—the side not yet stitched. Pivot and stitch down the other side, gradually increasing the width of the zigzag until the stitch reaches its original size.

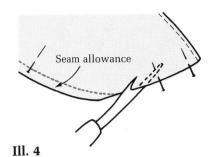

Ill. 3

Finishing. Take several stitches in place to end your stitching, whether to finish the project or just to change thread colors.

Cut the thread ends close to the fabric. Remove any stabilizer you may have used.

Hand appliqué

The whipstitch, running stitch, and blanket stitch are the most popular stitches to use in securing appliqués by hand. In all cases, the ¼-inch seam allowance is turned under along the appliqué edge as you go. Hand stitching finishes an appliqué beautifully, but it's time-consuming and not as durable as machine stitching.

The first step. Baste the first appliqué piece in place (see "Basting," on facing page), leaving the seam allowance flat.

Working 2 to 3 inches at a time along the edge of the appliqué piece, turn the seam allowance under. (A seam ripper makes the job easier—**Ill. 4**.) Insert pins perpendicular to the edge, 1 to 1½ inches apart.

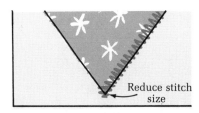

Seam allowance

Ill. 4

(Continued on page 42)

Start a thread as you would for embroidery (see page 26). With either the whipstitch or the running stitch, sew the pinned edge of the appliqué piece to the garment, using regular sewing thread and a size 8 or 9 quilting (betweens) needle. Or use the running stitch or the blanket stitch, sewing with embroidery floss or pearl cotton, and using a size 7 or 8 embroidery needle. Remove the pins as you sew.

Continue turning, pinning, and sewing the piece's edge in 2 to 3-inch sections. Tips on handling curves, corners, and points are included below. When you come to the end of a thread or a line of stitching, finish it as you would an embroidery thread (see page 26).

Stitching. Use any of the following stitches to secure your appliqué pieces to the garment.

● Whipstitch. This is a very secure stitch. Insert the needle in the garment fabric at the very edge of the appliqué piece and bring it up through the appliqué fabric, no more than ⅛ inch from the edge, taking a small diagonal stitch (**Ill. 5**). Reinsert it into the garment fabric a little farther along, and continue stitching.

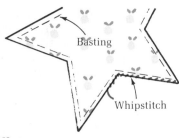

Ill. 5

● Running stitch. When worked in embroidery thread, this stitch is very decorative. See "Basic stitches" on page 26 for directions; take tiny stitches (¹⁄₁₆ to ⅛

inch long), no more than ⅛ inch from the edge of the appliqué.

● Blanket stitch. This stitch effectively outlines the appliqué shapes. See "Basic stitches" on pages 26–27 for directions.

Handling curves. Clip the seam allowance of a concave curve every ¼ to ½ inch before folding it, to ensure a smooth, flat edge (**Ill. 6**). Clip less than ¼ inch into the fabric. Strengthen the seam in a clipped area by placing the stitches very close together.

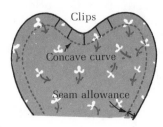

Ill. 6

To smooth the edges of convex curves, position your index and middle fingers on the folded edge and press down. Run the needle under the allowance, gently prodding excess fabric into evenly distributed folds (**Ill. 7**). Pin and then stitch the edge.

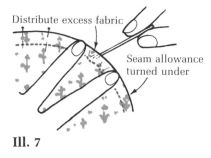

Ill. 7

Points & corners. To stitch a point, turn the seam allowance under along one side of the appliqué piece; stitch to within ½ inch of the end. Trim off the triangle protruding from under the appliqué piece (**Ill. 8**).

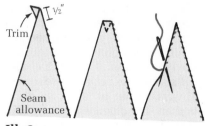

Ill. 8

Turn under ¼ inch of the piece's point as shown; stitch to the end of the first seam. Turn under the adjacent seam allowance and continue stitching, taking a few additional stitches as you round the folded point to help smooth the edges.

Use the same technique to stitch corners smoothly.

Appliqué variations

Enhance your appliqué work with some embroidery, quilting, or three-dimensional effects. The dramatic results will reap lots of applause.

Quilting. Outline-quilt your project around the appliqué to highlight the shape of the design. To emphasize design features, pad the shape using the trapunto technique. See "Trapunto" on page 50 for directions.

Embroidery. Add French knots to give dimension and texture. Use other embroidery stitches to add detail. See "Embroidery" on page 26 for directions.

Three-dimensional appliqué. By only partly attaching a shape to the garment fabric, you can give your appliqué a touch of whimsy. For example, make an apron for a doll appliqué by gathering a piece of fabric and stitching it to the doll's waistline. Or whipstitch an elephant ear so it flops as your toddler walks.

Your pick of patterns

There are countless places to find a design that's just perfect for your newest appliqué project. Don't feel restricted to using a design pattern only on the project on which it appears. For example, you can adjust the size of the appliqué designs for the "Animals-on-parade quilt" on page 70 and add them to a jacket, crib bumpers, or the knees of overalls. Other places to find designs suitable for children's clothes are coloring books, magazines, and greeting cards.

On this page, we've included the designs you see appliquéd on the jackets shown in the index (page 96) and on the overalls on the cover. The enlarging key under the appliqué grid enables you to make the designs the size they appear on the garments. You can make them larger or smaller to suit the needs of your project (see "How to transfer a design," page 38).

If you prefer to hand stitch the appliqués rather than using a machine satin stitch, add ¼-inch seam allowances to all of the designs.

The heart at the bottom corner of the page is an actual-size pattern for the heart pin shown on the cover. To use the heart as a stuffed pin or as a hand-stitched appliqué, add a ¼-inch seam allowance around the edge. Use the shape exactly as it appears for a machine appliqué project.

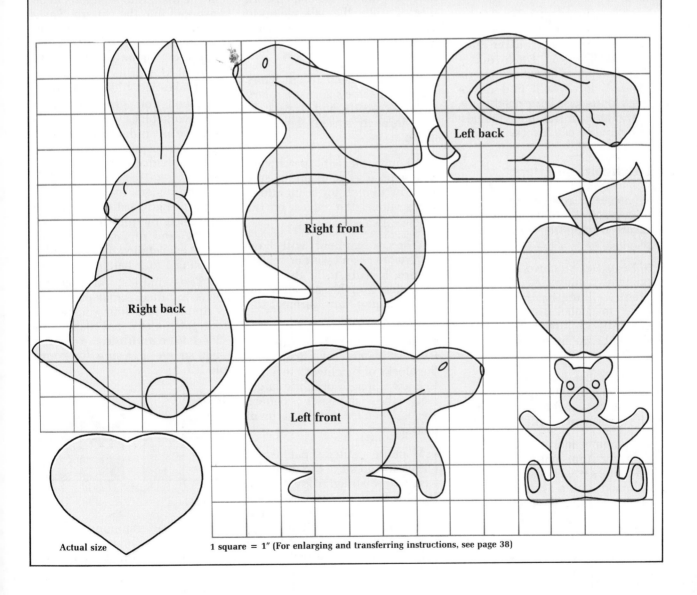

Left back

Right front

Right back

Left front

Actual size

1 square = 1″ (For enlarging and transferring instructions, see page 38)

Patchwork

Patchwork is the art of joining small pieces of fabric, such as rectangles, triangles, and squares, to form a geometric pattern within a block shape. Usually, blocks are then sewn together to form a continuous fabric with a repeating pattern.

Because of its nature, patchwork adapts easily to many different shapes and sizes. It works equally well as a narrow strip for borders or inserts, a full piece of fabric for an entire garment, or even as a single block for medallions or patches.

You can adapt many of the available patchwork patterns to children's wear. Refer to the *Sunset* book *Quilting, Patchwork & Appliqué* for specific pattern ideas. Below you'll find directions for making basic patchwork strips, and for the fundamentals of Seminole patchwork.

Patchwork pointers

Whatever type of patchwork you undertake, the hints below will assure trouble-free, professional results.

● Keep the patchwork patterns relatively simple, since children's clothing has fairly small areas to embellish. The basic piece in children's patchwork should be no more than 2 inches square.

● Match the fiber content and fabric weight of the patchwork as closely as possible to the fabric of the garment it will decorate.

● Combine fabrics in various light, medium, and dark colors. The colors you choose will evoke a mood—from lively crayon brights to romantic pastels.

● Select fabrics with varying scales of print. A combination of small, medium, and large prints will be much more interesting and pleasing than three polka dot fabrics in three colors. Key the prints to the size of the child, avoiding extremely large designs.

● Wash the fabrics before using them. Cut off both selvages before cutting the patchwork pieces.

● Accurate marking and cutting are essential to successful patchwork. A clear plastic ruler and triangle are excellent tools to have on hand for patchwork piecing, since they allow you to draw lines using previous markings and the fabric print as guidelines.

● When you need to cut many shapes the same size, use a rotary cutter. It neatly and accurately cuts through several layers of fabric at once.

● When a piece of patchwork will be used as an insert, be sure to allow ⅝ inch for seam allowances along the edges of the finished piece.

● When a garment will have patchwork as an insert or central feature, be sure to fit the insert accurately into the garment without changing any garment dimensions.

● When making an entire garment of patchwork, first piece the blocks of patchwork together to make a length of fabric larger than the garment's pattern pieces. Then cut out the garment pieces.

● Machine stitch patchwork pieces for greatest durability in wear and washing. Allow ¼-inch seams on all pieces; sew them using a medium-short stitch length (10 to 12 stitches per inch). When you're stitching strips to use in such techniques as the four-patch or Seminole, use a short stitch length (16 stitches per inch).

● Line patchwork garments to protect the seam allowances from fraying and pulling apart.

Patchwork in strips

Piecing patchwork patterns can become very time consuming. When the design allows, you can expedite the process by sewing long fabric strips together and cutting them into segments to be reworked into the pattern. Since children seem to grow faster than the time it takes to finish a demanding garment for them, any shortcut is worth looking into. All it takes is a little planning.

When you first look at a patchwork block, you may not perceive any order to the pattern, but closer inspection may reveal that it's divided into a number of smaller squares or triangles. These divisions make up a *grid pattern*. A grid pattern is easy to reproduce by piecing together, cutting, and repiecing strips of fabric as detailed below under "Making a four-patch."

The simplest grid-pattern block is called a *four-patch*—it is divided into four squares. A four-patch block may also be divided into multiples of four—eight squares to a side, for example (**Ill. 1**).

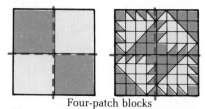

Four-patch blocks

Ill. 1

Another common block is called a *nine-patch*: it contains nine squares—three across and three down. In another version, each of the three squares is divided in quarters, creating six across and six down.

You can create any number of combinations by varying the size of the squares or by alternating the four-patch blocks with solid blocks of fabric.

Making a four-patch. Decide on the finished size of the squares in a block and add ¼ inch to each edge for seam allowances. A 2-inch finished square would be cut as a 2½-inch square.

Following the lengthwise grain, measure and cut each of two different fabrics into strips of your chosen width (2½ inches, to make 2-inch finished squares).

Sew two strips—one of each fabric—along one long edge, right sides together. Press the seam allowances to one side (toward the darker of the two fabrics, if they contrast greatly). Cut this strip into segments of your chosen length (2½ inches for a 2-inch finished square).

Invert one segment and pin it to another, right sides together, carefully aligning the center seams. Sew one edge and press the seams to one side to complete your four-patch block (**Ill. 2**). If the finished squares are 2 inches, the unfinished block will be 4½ inches square—4 inches when its edges are joined to other blocks.

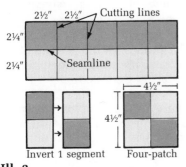

Ill. 2

(Continued on page 46)

A penchant for patchwork

Patchwork can liven anything—the edge of a vest, a hem, a cuff. Use it as an insert on a dress, bonnet, or overalls. Work it into fabric for a quilt, jacket, bib, baby bunting, or shirt yoke. A single patchwork block can appear as a medallion on the back of a shirt, and a single strip of patches can adorn each side front of a jacket.

You can make more blocks and join them together into larger blocks to create a large piece of fabric, or join them side by side to make a strip of fabric for borders and edges.

Making triangles. For variety, piece strips to make triangle shapes. Then piece the triangles into squares to use in the four-patch blocks, or into a single triangle row for a border design.

• *Triangle rows.* To make a single row of triangles, begin by stitching together strips of two different colors of fabric as described in "Making a four-patch," sewing at least four fabric strips together. Cut across the strips in segments and stitch the segments into a length of squares of alternating colors, like a checkerboard fabric (**Ill. 3**).

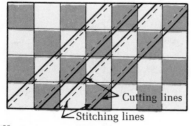

Ill. 3

Align your ruler so that it bisects a line of squares on the diagonal: mark this diagonal for one strip stitching line. Move to the next line of squares and mark the other seamline on the diagonal. Add ¼ inch outside each line for seam allowances, and mark the cutting lines (**Ill. 3**). Continue until the whole fabric is marked into strips of triangles; cut the strips.

• *Triangle squares.* Use the strip method to produce squares containing two different-colored triangles; it simplifies the process of piecing together a complex four or nine-patch block design.

To make the triangle squares, begin by measuring the diagonal of one of the finished squares in the block. (A 2-inch square, for example, has a 2⅞-inch diagonal.) Stitch a checkerboard of fabric strips as directed above for "Triangle rows," making the finished edge of each square equal to the diagonal of the squares in the finished block.

Mark and cut strips of triangles as directed above. Mark a line down the center of each triangle at right angles to the strip edge (**Ill. 4**). Cut along these lines; each segment will form a square of the correct size for use in your four or nine-patch block.

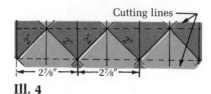

Ill. 4

Seminole patchwork

Seminole patchwork originated with the Florida Indians. It's a colorful variety of patchwork that looks terribly complex, yet is surprisingly simple (**Ill. 5**). It is best adapted for use as a strip insert in a garment.

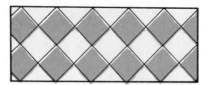

Ill. 5

The basic technique is much the same as the strip-piecing method for the four-patch, described above. Fabric strips are sewn together to make a piece of striped fabric, which is then cut into narrow striped segments. The narrow segments are sewn

together in a stair-step configuration to make a new design. The results are truly dramatic and intriguing.

Though books full of Seminole designs are available, we've provided one of the basic patterns to get you started. Once you've mastered the technique, you can invent variations by adding more strips of fabric, changing fabric widths, substituting different colors or cutting pieces diagonally, or adding mirror images. It's fun to experiment with endless permutations.

Whatever design you use, mark and cut the fabric strips along the grainline, making them ½ inch wider than the desired finished width. Make the strips as long as your fabric width. Bias tapes are particularly easy fabrics to use, since their edges are already folded to make ¼-inch seam allowances; the crease makes a handy guideline for stitching.

Always keep in mind that accurate and careful measurements are essential to the success of this technique. Follow the "Patchwork pointers" on page 44 for general directions.

Diamond Jubilee. This is a basic Seminole pattern—a good one to learn on. Cut three strips of fabric, each in a different color. Make the two outer strips 1½ inches wide and the center strip 1¼ inches wide. Stitch them together with ¼-inch seams; press the seams to one side.

Spread the fabric strip on a flat surface. At the left end of the strip, mark a line perpendicular to the long edges. Using this line as a guideline, mark divisions every 1¼ inches across the entire length of the strip. Cut the strip into pieces along these lines.

Pin the pieces together, aligning the lower edge of the

center color in each left-hand piece with the upper edge of the center color in each right-hand piece. Stitch the pieces together as you pin them, using ¼-inch seam allowances (**Ill. 6**). Each succeeding piece will form a stair-step with the previous one.

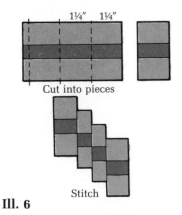

Cut into pieces

Stitch

Ill. 6

When you have completed a strip of fabric, turn it on its side so the pointed edges become the top and bottom. The center color will now appear in diamond shapes. To add a border to the Seminole strip or to stitch it to a garment, use the top and bottom points of the center-color diamonds as the markers for your final stitching lines (**Ill. 7**). When stitched in place, the patchwork strip is 1¼ inches deep and about 36 inches long. Trim the ends of the strip to straighten it.

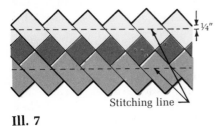

Stitching line

Ill. 7

Try variations of this design by adding more rows of color. Each new row adds at least ½

inch to the height of the strip, but won't have a noticeable effect on the length. Vary the width of the strips—enlarge them all or alternate narrow ones with wide ones.

● *Adding a border.* A border of contrasting fabric helps finish the edges of a Seminole patchwork strip and provides a frame for the work by separating it from the garment fabric. The border can be as wide as you wish, but should be no less than ¼ inch wide, plus ½ inch for seam allowances. (Remember to add the depth of these two borders to the finished depth of the patchwork when calculating the total dimension, especially if you're adding the piece to a garment.)

After cutting two border strips, mark lines ¼ inch outside the final stitching lines of the patchwork strip, on the upper and lower edges. Align the raw edge of a border strip with one of the drawn lines, *right* sides together; stitch a ¼-inch seam. The seam should run along the final stitching line of the patchwork piece. Repeat with the other border strip. Trim the edges of the patchwork piece even with the edges of the border seam allowances.

● *A new slant.* To vary the Diamond Jubilee pattern for a more exaggerated diamond effect, sew the three original strips of fabric together as directed above. Then use the following directions to cut the striped fabric diagonally, making slanted pieces of fabric.

Use a clear triangle to mark slanted lines at a 45-degree angle, marking the first line twice the width of the pieces to be cut. Make this mark along the top edge of the fabric for pieces that slant up to the right, along the bottom edge for pieces that slant up to the left.

Draw a line from the top or bottom of the guideline along the short edge (depending on your choice of right or left slant for the pieces) through the mark (**Ill. 8**). Continue to measure and mark pieces, using this line as your guideline. Then cut and sew these pieces as directed for Diamond Jubilee.

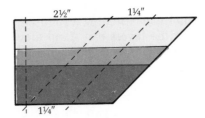

Ill. 8

● *Mirror image.* To make a dramatic chevronlike variation of the Diamond Jubilee pattern, using the slant-cut technique above, sew the three original strips of fabric together as directed for the Diamond Jubilee. Then fold the resulting strip in half and pin it, *wrong* sides together (**Ill. 9**). Mark the pieces off with diagonal lines as directed under "A new slant," above, and cut through both layers. When you turn all the pieces *right* side up, half of them will be mirror images of the other half. Sew them together, alternating slants and aligning the center color, using the directions for the Diamond Jubilee pattern, above.

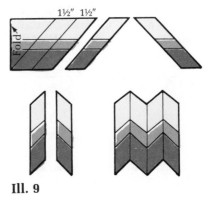

Ill. 9

Quilting

Does the word "quilt" conjure up cozy images of padded, handsomely stitched layers of fabric? Whether you prefer to quilt bed covers, buntings, overalls, or jackets, there's no limit to the stitching patterns you can use.

Quilting is the process of joining three layers of fabric: the top or *face*, the filling or *batting*, and the bottom or *backing*. The pattern of stitching you use to quilt the layers can stand alone as a design element or embellish the face fabric's print or design.

There are several ways to quilt fabric: the standard method of stitching the two fabric layers and the batting all at once like a sandwich; a variation called *trapunto*—stitching the fabric layers first and then stuffing batting only in specific areas; and tying—knotting the layers instead of stitching them.

Quilting designs

Before you start your standard quilting or trapunto project, give careful thought to your quilting design. Below are some options, ranging from simple to more complex. (See "Tied quilts," on page 51 for information on designing for that method.)

Background quilting. Background quilting designs fill an entire piece of fabric with simple repeating patterns of stitching, such as a grid, channels, a stair-step zigzag, or scallops (**Ill. 1**).

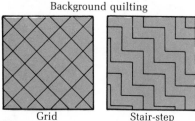

Background quilting

Grid   Stair-step

Ill. 1

Motif quilting. In motif quilting (also called ornamental quilting) the stitched design becomes a prominent feature. Designs—traditional, contemporary, or abstract—appear in medallion shapes or as running borders (**Ill. 2**). For children's clothes, choose relatively simple designs.

Motif quilting

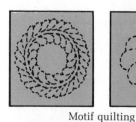

Ill. 2

Outline quilting. One or more lines of quilting stitches just outside the contours of a fabric print emphasize the print's shape (**Ill. 3**). This technique can also effectively highlight appliqué or patchwork on the face fabric.

Outline quilting

Ill. 3

Preparing to quilt

More is involved in preparing to quilt than just picking a pretty fabric.

Once you've chosen a face fabric, you'll need backing fabric and batting. Marking the stitching lines and basting the layers together are required work before you actually begin to quilt. The steps may seem lengthy, but they ensure successful results.

Fabric selection. Choose light to medium-weight, firmly woven fabrics, such as cottons or cotton blends, for clothing and quilts. Napped fabrics, such as velour or velveteen, are suitable if you use a simple quilting design.

Avoid oversize prints on the face fabric; they can overpower tiny bodies. The exception to this rule is certain large graphic prints that fit perfectly onto the back of a vest or around a bunting. You can create your own appliquéd, painted, printed, or patchwork face fabrics and use quilting to highlight their designs.

Select a lightweight, tightly woven fabric for the backing. Its care requirements should be similar to those of the face fabric.

Preshrink all fabrics before you quilt them.

Batting. For warmth and durability, use polyester batting instead of cotton batting as a quilt filler. Polyester batting is easy to stitch, and you can space your stitched quilting lines up to 4 inches apart without running the risk that the batting will shift over time.

Batting suitable for quilting ranges from a thin fleece to a high-loft variety. The higher the batting's loft, the more shrinkage you'll see in the quilt size when you stitch the layers together. A common choice for clothes and quilts is ¼-inch batting. It's available by the yard or in precut packages.

Marking. In most cases, the quilting lines must be marked on the face fabric before you begin to baste, to indicate your design. To transfer your design lines to the fabric, see "How to transfer a design" on page 38. Unless your design must be centered on a garment (see below), mark, baste, and quilt your entire yardage before cutting the garment fabric pieces.

Marking isn't necessary on patchwork fabric; you usually use the seamlines of the patchwork pieces as quilting lines. Likewise, when outline-quilting a fabric print or appliqué, follow the design contour instead of drawing lines.

If you're machine quilting a repeating pattern with parallel lines, or a grid, and you have a quilting guide attachment, you need to mark only the first line. Set the guide equal to the distance between the rows. When you stitch, you'll use the quilting guide to follow the contours of the previous stitching line (**Ill. 4**).

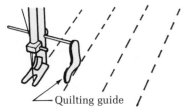

Quilting guide

Ill. 4

If your quilting design must be centered on parts of the garment, as in outline or motif quilting, you'll need to mark each garment fabric piece separately. Begin by positioning and pinning each pattern piece to your fabric; baste around the pattern edges to mark them.

Then remove the pattern and cut the fabric at least 2 inches outside the basted outline. Cen-

ter and mark the quilting design inside this area with a transfer pencil. After you quilt each fabric piece, reposition the pattern piece over it, centering the pattern over the quilted design, and cut the fabric to the pattern size. You'll find that the original basted outlines will seem to have shrunk, drawn in by the quilting stitches.

Basting. Basting the three fabric layers together before quilting is essential to the success of your project. If you don't baste, puckering and shifting will run rampant when you quilt.

On a smooth, flat surface, layer first the backing, right side *down*; then the batting; and finally the face fabric, right side *up*. Make sure they're all flat and smooth—wrinkles that get basted in will live forever. Pin the layers to hold them in place.

Use basting thread or a thread in a pale contrasting color to hand baste the layers in long running stitches.

Baste in straight lines, creating a radiating pattern, rather than following your marked quilting lines. Begin each line of basting at the center of the fabric; work toward the edges (**Ill. 5**). First complete a horizontal line, next a vertical line, and then the diagonals. The finished basting lines shouldn't be more than 4 inches apart to ensure smooth quilting.

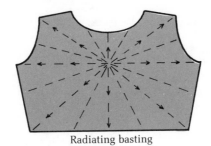

Radiating basting

Ill. 5

Quilting stitches

Standard quilting can be done by hand or machine. Since children's clothes and crib quilts will be washed frequently and worn hard, machine quilting is the better choice—it's quicker and more durable.

Machine quilting. Practice machine quilting on a basted sample of your face, batting, and backing fabric. Keep your practice stitching patterns open and not very intricate.

To stitch repeating lines and simple outlines, adjust the stitch length on your sewing machine to 8 to 10 stitches per inch. Loosen the thread tension and presser foot pressure slightly. Use a small-hole throat plate and a clear presser foot, if your machine has them.

To prevent puckers, always stitch in one direction, working from center to edges of fabric.

To machine quilt a motif or intricate pattern outline, use freehand machine embroidery techniques (see page 24); they'll let you maneuver the fabric layers easily (**Ill. 6**).

Freehand quilting

Ill. 6

To start and stop stitching, take a few stitches in place, then clip the thread ends close to the fabric.

(Continued on page 50)

Three-dimensional fabric

Quilting—here and there, or everywhere on a garment—adds dimension and warmth and an extra touch of texture. Use it to outline an appliqué, patchwork, or large graphic print. Use quilting alone to add a pattern to solid-color fabric. Try tied quilting to make a winsome, puffy jacket. Or let a touch of trapunto turn an ordinary garment into one that's simply smashing.

Hand quilting. To hand quilt, stretch the face, batting, and backing in a hoop and stitch through all three layers.

Always work from the center of the fabric toward the edges, to prevent puckers or shifting. Use an 18-inch length of quilting thread, knotted at one end. Pull the knot into the batting to conceal it.

To stitch, rock your hand in a slight up-and-down movement, taking three or four short running stitches at a time through all the layers.

To end the thread, make a single looped knot about ¼ inch from the quilt face. Insert the needle into the face close to where the thread last emerged, and slip the needle horizontally through the batting and up through the face again. Tug gently on the thread until the knot pops into the batting; cut the thread close to the quilt face.

Trapunto

Trapunto is the technique of outlining motifs with stitches and then stuffing them for a padded, sculptural effect. You stitch only the two layers of fabric together, without batting between. Then you pad the stitched areas with loose batting or yarn.

For the face, use a light to medium-weight, firmly woven fabric. A lightweight fabric such as muslin or voile is best for the backing. You'll need to line a trapunto garment to protect the stitched openings in the backing fabric.

Stuffed trapunto. This technique is great for highlighting part of a fabric print or appliqué, or for adding dimension and texture to a motif without using batting throughout the whole garment.

Transfer your quilting design to the face fabric and mark, cut, and baste the garment pieces as directed on pages 48–49 for outline and motif quilting, under "Preparing to quilt."

Stitch the design by hand or machine, following the instructions in "Quilting stitches," pages 49–50. You can stitch just the design's outline, or add more stitching to shape details. For example, you might only outline-stitch a duckling, but for a swan, you'd add stitching to define the head, wing, and feathers (**Ill. 7**).

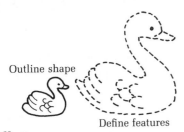

Outline shape

Define features

Ill. 7

When the design is completely stitched, cut a small slit in the backing, within each design area enclosed by stitching. Be sure to cut *only* the backing fabric, not the face. Using a blunt needle or crochet hook, insert a small amount of batting between the layers (**Ill. 8**).

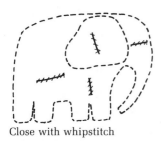

Close with whipstitch

Ill. 8

Continue adding stuffing to each stitched part of the design until the motif is smooth and puffy. Don't overstuff—it creates puckers and distortion.

Corded trapunto. Traditionally used to highlight a motif, corded trapunto makes a beautiful play of shadow and light through the subtlety of raised outlines. These raised lines can also delineate a repeating pattern or stripes.

To prepare for corded trapunto, mark, cut, and baste your fabric pieces as in "Stuffed trapunto" on facing page. When you stitch the design, using the directions under "Quilting stitches" (pages 49–50), stitch two parallel lines, ⅛ to ⅜ inch apart, instead of one line (**Ill. 9**). The two lines create a channel into which you'll insert cording.

Trapunto channels

Ill. 9

Thread a blunt tapestry needle with a single or double length of washable yarn or cotton cording. Working through the backing, carefully insert the needle between the two layers at the beginning of the design (**Ill. 10**).

Yarn

Ill. 10

Run the needle through the stitched channel, bringing it out where the design curves or turns a corner. Insert the needle again and continue, leaving a little extra yarn out at each turn to prevent puckering. Be careful not to catch any face fabric in your nee-

dle. At the start and finish, trim the yarn ends close to the fabric, and work them into the holes.

Tied quilts

Tying is a quick and easy technique for holding a sandwich of fabric and batting layers. It maintains a billowy loft because, unlike stitching, the widely spaced knots don't compress the batting.

Prepare your fabric layers as described in "Preparing to quilt," above. Decide where the knots will work best in the overall scheme of the quilting. For example, if your face fabric is patchwork, tie the corner of each block along the seamlines, or tie through the center of each block.

Space the knots no more than 6 inches apart. On small garments, maintain proportion by spacing knots no farther than 3 to 4 inches apart.

Tying knots. Use a long needle with a double length of durable yarn, pearl cotton, or crochet thread to knot the quilt layers.

Always start from the center of the basted layers and work toward the edges. Insert the needle from the face through to the backing, drawing the yarn through and leaving a 2-inch tail on the face.

Bring the needle back up to the face and cut the yarn, leaving another 2-inch tail. Tie the two tails in a square knot, left tail over right, then right tail over left (**Ill. 11**). Trim the ends evenly.

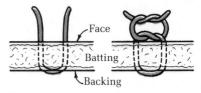

Face

Batting

Backing

Ill. 11

Painting

Use fabric as your canvas and paint directly on it to create exciting designs on your children's clothes, toys, or room decorations. It's surprisingly simple to master the technique, and there's no need to worry that your artwork will fade in the wash—it's permanent.

Sewing skill isn't a prerequisite for fabric painting. You can paint designs on finished garments almost as easily as on uncut fabric yardage.

Choose your medium: fabric pigment paints and dyes, fabric pigment crayons, or indelible ink markers. Apply them in freehand designs or stenciled patterns, or stamp them on—directions follow.

Whatever method of painting you choose, keep the design simple. Coloring books or posters with simple shapes are a good source of design ideas. Think big: paint a design up the leg of a pair of overalls and carry it right onto the bib (**Ill. 1**), or cover an entire wall banner.

Use fabric as a paint canvas

Ill. 1

Small is beautiful, too—paint some little shapes across the yoke of a jumper, on a pocket, or around a baby's bib (**Ill. 2**). The smaller your paintbrush, the more detail you can add to your design.

Use delicate art in tiny places

Ill. 2

Setting up to paint

Prepare a work area, gathering all the necessary tools and supplies so they're at your fingertips before you start to paint. Fabric paints are water soluble until heat set, so soapy water is all you need to clean brushes and equipment, as well as your skin. But cover your work surface and your clothes to protect them from splatters, especially if your children are going to join you in this creative adventure.

Work surface. Cover a piece of cardboard with plastic or acetate and place it under the fabric you're going to paint. If you're working on a finished garment, such as a T-shirt or a jacket, slide the plastic-covered board between the fabric layers. Pin the garment to the cardboard to keep the fabric smooth and taut while you work.

Paint, stamp, or stencil your fabric according to the directions below. Leave the fabric on the board while the paint dries; the board will help set the paint.

Fabric. You can paint a length of fabric before cutting and sewing it into a project, or paint directly onto a ready-made garment. Wash any fabric you purchase before you paint it.

A woven or knit fabric of cotton or cotton/polyester blend, of any weight, will give the best color resolution from the paint. A 65 percent cotton/35 percent polyester blend is best, but you can use a fabric with as much as 50 percent polyester. Avoid other synthetic fabrics; they won't retain the high color intensity that these fibers will.

Choose white or a pale pastel fabric if you don't want the fabric color to interfere with your paint colors.

If you want to paint within specific design lines, transfer the design to the fabric before you start painting, using the directions under "How to transfer a design" on page 38.

Paint. Fabric paints are made of pigments that actually dye the fabric when and where they're applied. Once the paint is set with heat, it permanently impregnates the fabric and won't wash out or wear off.

All types of fabric paint come with manufacturer's directions for application and cleanup.

Artist's acrylic paints aren't recommended for children's clothes. Once dry, they form a crust on fabric that can flake off; in addition, they require dry cleaning. But acrylics are useful for painting shoes or other accessories—to carry a particular color or design to all parts of a child's wardrobe.

Direct painting

Painting is the easiest and quickest way to enhance fabric. Using motifs ranging from simple abstract paint strokes and repeating patterns to elaborate murals, you can make your own patterned fabric for any purpose.

Use artist's brushes to apply fabric paint. If you want a bold stroke, use a large brush.

Place a small amount of each paint color in a white plastic bubble tray—the type used for water colors (**Ill. 3**). If you expose large amounts of paint or work directly from an open paint jar, your paint will dry out.

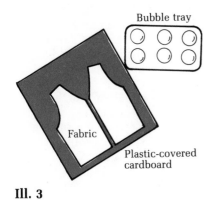

Ill. 3

Mix paints to create any color or intensity you want. Add extender or water for a paler, water-color look.

If your design calls for clean, sharp lines at the edges of each painted area, place masking tape along those edges before you begin to paint. The tape will prevent the paint from seeping through, and there'll be a sharp edge when it's removed (**Ill. 4**).

Masking tape guideline

Ill. 4

Use the masking tape technique to keep the edges between adjoining colors sharp, but don't apply the tape to a painted area until the paint is completely dry.

Hesitant to put the first line of paint on your fabric? Loosen up by trying your hand on some scrap fabric—you'll soon be eager to get to your project, and then to another, and another.

Once you've finished painting a project, let the paint dry thoroughly before lifting the fabric from the plastic-covered surface. Then heat-set the painted surface to fix the colors permanently: with a dry iron, press the fabric, using the paint manufacturer's directions for temperature and time.

Stamping

Stamps can be made from practically anything you have on hand. They're easy to use, so let your preschoolers join in the fun.

Repeating shapes in single file can add a final touch around a garment's hem, yoke, cuffs, or bib. Or watch a bigger and bigger design grow as you stamp large areas of fabric.

Below, you'll find a variety of common stamp-making materials to choose from—and you may want to invent your own.

When you make stamps, remember that the pattern you cut will appear as a mirror image when stamped onto fabric. If you have a one-way design, such as one using letters and numbers, be sure to cut it backwards (**Ill. 5**).

Potato stamp

Ill. 5

To prepare for stamping, spread fabric paint on a piece of aluminum foil or a cooky sheet. Use a plastic-covered piece of cardboard underneath the fabric, as described on the facing page in "Setting up to paint." Stamp the paint over the fabric, pressing firmly to ensure adequate paint transfer. Let it dry before moving the fabric. Heat-set the painted surface as described in "Direct painting," at left.

Potato stamps. These are age-old stamping tools. To make one, cut a potato crosswise and mark your design in pencil on the cut surface. With an art knife or narrow kitchen knife, cut away any part of the potato that isn't within the design lines, making a raised surface for your print.

Foam. The foam you use to fill mats or cushions makes a good stamping surface. Cut the foam into shapes with scissors, and glue each shape to a piece of heavy cardboard or acrylic to make a backing and handle (**Ill. 6**).

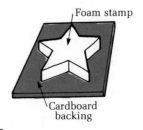

Foam stamp

Cardboard backing

Ill. 6

Rubber stamps. Those wonderful stamps you see in stationery stores make good fabric-paint stamps. Just spread fabric paint onto an uninked stamp pad and press the stamp into the pad to pick up paint. Use a piece of rubber foam as a pad if you can't locate an uninked stamp pad.

(Continued on page 54)

Stenciling

Stencils make repeating patterns that are quick and easy to complete. Whether the motif is galloping horses or entwined flowering vines, professional-looking results are yours with very little effort when you use stencils. Make your own designs (see below), or purchase ready-made stencils in fabric, craft, or art supply stores.

To prepare for stenciling, follow the guidelines in "Setting up to paint," page 52. Stretch your fabric over the plastic-covered cardboard; tape it in place with masking tape to prevent it from slipping. Also tape your stencil in place on the fabric.

Handling the paint. A special stencil fabric paint is available—it's like fabric paint, but thicker. Its thickness prevents it from running or smearing under the stencil cutout and from drying out if you use it directly from the jar.

The thickness also keeps the paint from permeating the wrong side of the fabric. This is quite a plus when you want to paint on finished garments, especially those with linings.

You'll need only a small amount of paint at a time. Don't be tempted to use too much; it will bleed through the fabric. To apply the paint, use a stencil brush with a thick set of bristles, cut bluntly across the bottom. Apply paint either by pouncing the brush (tapping it directly against the fabric) or by using a circular motion, working from the outer edge of each shape toward the center.

Work with one stencil and one paint color at a time. After you've filled in all the spaces on one stencil, let the paint set for a few minutes before removing the stencil. Then align and tape the next stencil, using the registration marks for accurate placement. Be careful not to smudge the paint; it's thick and may take some time to dry.

Once the paint is dry, heat-set the stenciled fabric, using the method described in "Direct painting," page 52.

Making a stencil. You can create or adapt any design you want to make your own stencil.

Stencil paper is inexpensive and will withstand repeated use. But you might consider using acetate instead—its transparency makes it easy to position on the fabric, and it's especially useful when you have multiple layers of stencils.

Trace your design onto stencil paper, using the techniques in "How to transfer a design" on page 38, or trace it on acetate, using a felt-tip pen. Use a different stencil layer for each color in the design.

Cut the stencil with an art knife, working over a heavy cardboard or glass surface.

Use registration marks to line up each repeating design or different-color stencil (**Ill. 7**).

Design drawn on graph paper

First sheet of acetate

Cut
stencil
design

Second sheet of acetate

Registration marks

Ill. 7

Adhesive stencils. Letter and numeral stencils on adhesive paper are available in various sizes. They can be used in either of the two ways described below.

In the first method, cut the background adhesive evenly between letters to make rectangles with a letter in the center of each; pull a background rectangle away from its backing and apply it to the fabric. Mark a guideline on the fabric for straight placement of each letter. Use the spacing dots on the stencils or space each letter evenly according to your own specifications.

Fill the letter space with paint. After the paint has set for a few minutes, remove the adhesive. You'll have a clearly defined letter painted onto your fabric (**Ill. 8**).

Adhesive
background

Ill. 8

To use the second method, apply the adhesive letters themselves to the fabric along marked guidelines (see above). Affix all the letters before you begin to paint. Draw a design around them and apply masking tape to the design edges as directed under "Direct painting," page 52, to keep the edges sharp when painted. Paint over the letters, filling in the design. After the paint has set for a few minutes, lift the letters. You'll have letters the color of your fabric, surrounded by a paint color (**Ill. 9**).

Adhesive letter

Ill. 9

Alternatives to paint

Besides fabric paint, there are several other ways to color designs on fabric. Fabric-marking crayons and indelible-ink markers are two examples.

Fabric crayons. Children especially enjoy using fabric crayons—they look just like wax ones. Look for iron-on crayons or pastel dye sticks in art supply stores, hobby shops, or fabric stores.

Follow the manufacturer's directions for coloring and heat-setting the crayon or pastel designs.

Felt markers. Use indelible felt-tipped markers to add highlights or details—such as whiskers on a cat's face or rosy cheeks on a stuffed doll—to painted or appliquéd designs.

Also use markers to draw on small areas of fabric, such as socks, tights, collars, and cuffs.

Heat-setting isn't necessary to make indelible ink permanent. Once you've marked your fabric, the line is there to stay. These markers are best kept out of reach of children.

Paint a pretty picture

Kids love color, and with fabric paints you can add it with abandon. Whether you brush it, stamp it, or stencil it, fabric paint adds glorious colors with amazing ease. From head to toe, hair ribbons to sneakers, on bibs, buntings, overalls, shirts, skirts, and jackets—everything becomes a canvas for fabric paints.

Dyeing fabric

Plain knit shirts and socks, or even canvas coveralls take on a whole new life when they're dyed in vibrant colors. Hand-me-downs that look faded and sad turn bright and exciting after a dyebath in your child's favorite color.

Clothes made of natural fibers, such as cotton and wool, absorb and retain color intensity better than synthetics. Fiber blends are also suitable, but 100 percent synthetics may not hold a color satisfactorily.

Dyeing techniques

Though several types of fabric dye are available, they're basically either hot-water or cold-water dye. Check the package to be sure the dye you choose provides the best color absorption and is safest for your fabric.

Whatever dye you choose, follow the manufacturer's directions carefully, and let the hints below lead you to successful results.

● If possible, use a fabric scrap to test the fabric's ability to retain the dye. To see how the color sets, let the scrap dry; it will be a lighter shade dry than it was wet.

● Wash new fabrics before dyeing them, to remove any finishes that might inhibit the dyeing process. Also wash used garments to remove spots or soil.

● Protect yourself with rubber gloves and a smock.

● To create different colors, mix dye solutions according to package directions. Also take your fabric color into account: any color already on the garment will combine with the dye to produce a third color. For example, a light yellow shirt dyed in blue dye will turn green.

More dyeing ideas

It isn't necessary to dye an entire garment uniformly in order to change its color. You can paint with dye, using as many colors as you like; you can inhibit color absorption with wax; or you can dip the garment repeatedly into the dye for graded shades of color.

Painting. Paint dye solution directly onto fabric just as you would fabric paints (see "Direct painting" on page 52). Though the technique is the same, the results may be slightly different.

Dye solution is thinner than fabric paint; when it penetrates the fabric, it migrates slightly into the neighboring fibers. The edges of a line painted with dye will be soft and fuzzy, rather than sharp.

Use this softness to your advantage when designing your dye-painted pattern. Neighboring colors will blend with each other, creating a third color.

When it's dry, heat-set the dyed fabric to make the dye permanent. Follow the directions under "Direct painting," page 52.

Resist dyeing. The *resist method* is a batik variation, involving the application of wax to create a design (**Ill. 1**). Any area of fabric you cover with wax before dyeing will remain uncolored after the dye is applied and the wax is removed.

Melt paraffin and apply it to the fabric, covering the areas you don't want dyed. Use an inexpensive natural-bristle paintbrush; you'll discard it when your project is complete.

Once the wax dries, paint your design on the fabric with dye, following the directions in "Direct painting" on page 52. The waxed areas will repel any dye applied to them.

Let the dye dry thoroughly. To remove the wax, sandwich the fabric between layers of newsprint and press with a hot, dry iron for about 20 seconds to melt the wax out of the fabric. The newsprint will absorb almost all the melted wax. Wash the fabric to remove any wax residue.

Ombré colors. A subtle flow from a light to a dark shade of color—the French call it *ombré*—is easily obtained by repeatedly dipping fabric in dye. Rubber gloves are particularly important for this technique.

Submerge the entire garment or length of fabric in the dyebath for just a few minutes. Remove and rinse the fabric according to the dye manufacturer's directions. Repeat the dyeing process several times, each time dipping less of the garment into the dyebath (**Ill. 2**).

Ill. 1

Ill. 2

Young artists' gallery

As soon as they can hold a marker, children are fascinated with the art they create. Their early random lines and shapes progress into primitive figures.

Through their artwork, you can see the amazing development of children's muscle control and coordination and their perception of the surrounding world.

Keep those treasured dabblings permanently on display—preserve them on fabric, using such thread or fabric techniques as embroidery or appliqué. Or let your budding artists create directly on fabric with fabric paints or markers.

You can make aprons, jackets, book bags, pillows, or even quilt squares with your new "designer" fabric (**Ill. 1**). Or you can use it to adorn finished garments, sheets, or curtains—adding new life to simple backgrounds.

Ill. 1

Art in a new medium

Your children hurry home from nursery school or day care and proudly present their artwork of the day. But—horrors—you've run out of space on the refrigerator gallery. What to do? Try immortalizing the art by transferring it to a garment or piece of fabric via hand or machine embroidery, appliqué, or fabric paint.

Follow the instructions in "How to transfer a design," on page 38, to enlarge or reduce the drawing to fit the intended project, and to transfer the basic lines of the art onto the fabric. Then follow this book's instructions dealing with the medium of your choice.

Whatever your medium, be sure your rendition captures the whimsy and color of the original drawing. Let your young artist have some influence in the fabric makeover by choosing the thread or fabric colors.

Use further techniques to embellish the new fabric art. For example, add dimension to an appliqué with quilting, or enhance it with embroidered details (**Ill. 2**).

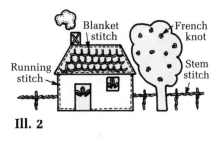

Ill. 2

Painting on a fabric canvas

It's a rainy day and the children are quickly losing interest in their crayon-and-paper drawings. Replace the paper with fabric and the crayons with fabric paint or fabric crayons. Along with gleeful children, absorbed in their work, you'll be rewarded with some very special custom-designed fabric.

Rarely is inspiration an obstacle, but a child's ability may be. Understand your child's artistic capabilities and tailor your project to them.

Toddlers may not draw specific shapes, but they're masters of the squiggly lines that soon become wonderful abstract patterns, full of color and movement. They can also manipulate stamps made of potato, foam, or rubber. Preschoolers can handle paintbrushes and fabric crayons, as well as simple stencil designs.

The "Painting" instructions on pages 52–55 will give you ideas and information on fabric paints and how to handle them on fabric.

Carefully cover any surface in the work area that you don't want painted, including the children's clothing. Secure a stretched length of fabric to a covered floor, table, or wall.

For painting or stenciling, place a small amount of each paint color in a saucer, and supply large-handled brushes to work with. Children can dip their paintbrushes into assorted colors and splatter the fabric with dots and splashes.

For even freer forms, spread the paint onto a cooky sheet, so toddlers can dip their hands into it and fingerpaint or fingerprint.

Let children design their own potato stamps, and help them cut out the shapes. Then let them freely experiment, stamping designs in different colors all over the fabric.

Stencils are another way for children to manipulate paint into a neatly defined design. Make the stencil shapes simple and relatively large (at least 4 inches in diameter).

Children can place the stencils where they please and spread the paint over the design. Once the paint is dry and the stencils removed, they can decorate any remaining spaces.

Projects

A bounty of bibs

Making clothes for children can be more fun than you ever imagined. Their garment designs have simple lines that make for fast and simple sewing and allow lots of room for personalizing.

Then there's the bonus of whimsy: you can let your imagination run wild when you sew children's clothes. Who but a child would dare to dance in a pair of bear paws (page 60)? And bibs (at right) are a good place to free your decorative fancy.

Since boys and girls up to age six have the same body types, their clothing patterns are interchangeable. The colors, patterns, embellishments, or trims you use will personalize each item you make. For example, the jacket or vest on page 62 gains its character from the trims you use to decorate it. Let your child help choose the fabric and trims; it'll be a rewarding experience for both of you.

Choose machine washable and dryable fabrics for all children's clothes. Preshrink all fabrics before you begin a garment.

For each project that follows, a reduced pattern appears on a grid. Enlarge the pattern, following the instructions in "How to transfer a design" on page 38.

Here are three easy bib patterns you can personalize with trims from rickrack to ribbons, or with enhancements from cross stitch to patchwork; see pages 24–57 for embellishment ideas.

Just about any firmly woven fabric can be used for a bib, as long as it's machine washable. For double mileage, make the bibs reversible by using a backing fabric with a texture or print that contrasts with the front fabric.

You'll need . . .

Circular bib—11½" diameter:
- ⅓ yard fabric
- ⅓ yard medium-weight interfacing (optional)
- ¾ yard piping
- ¾ yard wide single-fold bias tape

Rectangular bib—10 by 15":
- ½ yard fabric
- ½ yard medium-weight interfacing (optional)
- 2 yards wide single-fold bias tape

Bib with pocket—12" long:
- ½ yard vinyl fabric
- 2¼ yards double-fold bias tape

Note: The yardage listed will accommodate several bib pieces; depending on the width of your fabric, you'll be able to make from two to four complete bibs.

Circular bib

1 Enlarge pattern pieces A (bib) and B (ruffle) to full size, using grid scale. Cut fabric pieces as directed on grid (cut one of the A pieces in a contrasting fabric, if desired); add any embellishments.

2 Cut two A pieces from interfacing, if desired. Baste interfacing to wrong side of each bib piece.

3 Pin piping to right side of bib front, ½ inch from outer edge. Using a zipper presser foot, baste along piping stitching line (see page 34).

4 Stitch ruffle strips together along short end, ¼ inch from raw edge; press seam allowances open. Fold strip in half lengthwise, wrong sides together. With a long machine stitch, stitch ⅜ inch from raw edges; pull bobbin thread to gather fabric.

5 With raw edges matching, pin ruffle to right side of bib front along outer edge, spacing gathers to fit; baste ⅜ inch from edge.

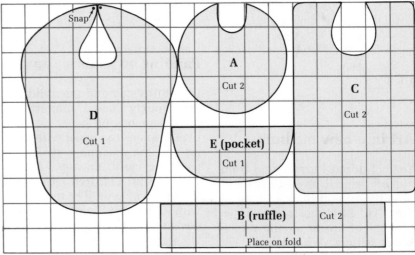

1 square = 1″ (For enlarging and transferring instructions, see page 38)
Seam allowances included

6 Pin bib back piece to front, right sides together. With bib front on top, stitch around outer edge, just inside piping basting stitches. Turn bib right side out; press. Baste opening closed.

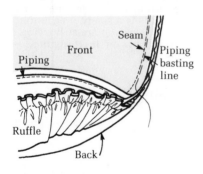

7 Press short ends of bias tape ¼ inch to wrong side. Matching center of neck to center of bias tape, encase neck edge of bib with bias tape, as described in "Encasing a raw edge," page 33. Stitch from one end of bias tape to the other, creating ties at the same time you finish neck edge.

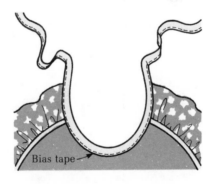

Rectangular bib

1 Enlarge pattern piece C to full size, using grid scale. Cut two fabric pieces, one in a contrasting fabric, if desired; add any embellishments.

2 Cut two C pieces from interfacing, if desired. Baste interfacing to wrong side of each fabric piece.

3 Pin front and back bib pieces, right sides together; stitch ½ inch from edge, leaving neck edge open. Turn right side out; press.

4 Cut a 44-inch piece of bias tape to encase neck edge of bib, following Circular Bib Step 7.

Optional: Encase outer edges of bib, as described in "Encasing a raw edge," page 33.

Bib with pocket

1 Enlarge pattern pieces D (bib) and E (pocket) to full size, using grid scale. Cut fabric pieces.

2 Using the topstitched application described in "Encasing a raw edge," page 33, encase straight edge of pocket with bias tape. Pin *wrong* side of pocket to *right* side of bib; stitch ¼ inch from edge, leaving top edge of pocket open.

3 Using the same topstitched application as in Step 2, encase outer edges of bib and neck edge with bias tape.

4 Sew snap to bib neck at marks.

Design: Tricia Bourdakis.

Animal slippers

Usually slippers are quickly forgotten and banished to the back of the closet. Not so with these friendly faces! One basic pattern helps you create a pair of lambs, cats, frogs, or bear paws that are sure to please the most discerning little feet.

You'll need . . .

To make one pair of slippers:

½ yard fabric (Use machine washable fake fur for cats and bear paws, fake fleece for lambs, corduroy for frogs.)

10 by 45-inch lightweight lining fabric

¼-inch-thick batting

1 package grip-fabric (sold for pajama bottoms)

4 black ball buttons* *(for lamb, cat, or frog eyes)*

White satin scrap *(for frog eyes)*

Synthetic suede scrap *(for bear claws or lamb ears)*

White fur scrap *(for cat ears)*

2 small pompons *(for cat noses)*

Dental floss *(for cat whiskers)*

*For infants and young toddlers, you may prefer to make embroidered eyes (using black satin stitches) instead of sewing on buttons. This is a safety precaution for children who are still trying to pull or chew on anything tuggable.

Stitching the slippers

Note: Stitch ¼-inch seams throughout.

1 Outline child's foot on paper. Measure length of foot and add 1 inch. Divide number of inches by 6 to determine size of your pattern grid squares. (Example: Child's foot is 4¼ inches long. Adding 1 inch equals 5¼ inches; dividing by 6 equals 0.875 [or ⅞] inch.) Make grid squares ⅞ inch for all pattern pieces, or round up to 1 inch if your child is growing quickly. Draw grid and transfer each pattern piece from grid below.

2 Cut fabric pieces, as follows: Cut 2 Tops from fake fur or fabric, and 2 Tops from lining. (*To make frog, also cut 2 Tops from batting.*) To cut fake fur, pin pattern pieces to wrong side of fabric; cut backing only, avoiding cutting into the pile.

Cut 2 Soles each from grip-fabric, batting, and Top fabric, reversing pattern for right and left foot.

For frog eyes, lamb ears, and cat ears, cut 2 of the 4 pieces from a contrasting fabric (see materials list above for suggestions).

3 For each slipper, pin Top fabric and lining, right sides together. Stitch around inside curve; clip seam. If using fake fur, carefully pull hair ends from seam to avoid flattened ridge at seamline.

For frog Top, baste batting to wrong side of fabric and work with fabric and batting as one piece. Trim batting seam allowance close to seam.

4 Press seam allowances open. With lining pulled away from fabric, stitch back seam as shown in illustration below.

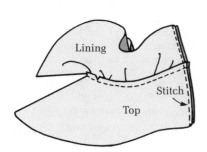

5 Baste the 3 Sole layers together—grip-fabric, right side down; then batting; then slipper fabric, right side up.

6 With slipper inside out, pin Sole to Top, holding edge of Top lining away from seam; stitch around outside edge. Slipstitch lining to Sole, enclosing seam allowance.

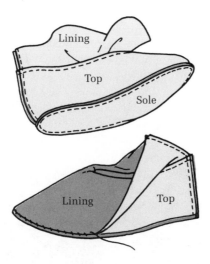

7 Turn slippers right side out. Stitch-in-the-ditch (see Glossary, page 9) at back seam to prevent lining from slipping.

8 *For frog eyes, cat ears, and lamb forehead,* stitch pieces, right sides together, leaving bottom edges open. *For bear claws,* fold each piece with right side inside; stitch along straight edge.

Turn pieces right side out and stuff with batting. Turn raw edges ¼ inch to inside and slipstitch pieces to slippers.

For lamb ears, blanket stitch suede and fleece pieces, wrong sides together. Slipstitch to slippers.

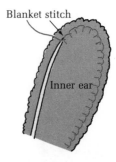

9 *Sew button eyes (and cat noses)* in place with heavy-duty thread. (Or embroider eyes, using a satin stitch with 3 strands black embroidery floss.)

Make cat whiskers by threading a 4-inch piece of dental floss through Top; tie ends in a square knot. Do this twice on each side of nose. Trim whiskers to desired length.

Design: Françoise Kirkman.

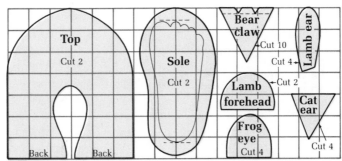

1 square = length of foot + 1″ ÷ 6   ¼″ seam allowance included
(For enlarging and transferring instructions, see page 38)

Wardrobe toppers: Jackets & vests

From one simple pattern, you can make a wardrobe of jackets and vests for boys and girls. Add sleeves for a jacket; leave them off for a vest. Use a center or asymmetric opening, with ties or buttons to lock in warmth.

You'll need . . .

    1 yard quilted fabric or
        medium to heavyweight
        nonquilted fabric

    1½ yards wide bias tape

    ¼ yard fabric for front band

    1 yard lining fabric (optional)

Making the pattern

1 Determine the appropriate size pattern by measuring around the child's chest when he or she is fully dressed; add 2 inches to this measurement. Pattern sizes are shown at the top of the next column; if your child's measurement is in between two sizes, use the larger size.

Size 1: 23″ chest   Size 4: 27″ chest
Size 2: 25″ chest   Size 6: 29″ chest

2 Enlarge the pattern using the grid scale (see page 38); then make any necessary adjustments for size on the full-size pattern (see chart on facing page).

Optional: To make an asymmetric closing, first cut the back and front Jacket patterns apart at the shoulder line, and add ½-inch seam allowances to all shoulder edges. Then redraw *one* front closing by moving front edge 2 inches past original line. Extend diagonal neck edge to intersect new front edge.

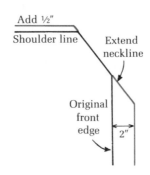

Making the jacket

Note: If you don't line the jacket, stitch flat-fell seams (page 16).

1 Cut fabric pieces as directed on grid, and add any embellishments (see pages 24–57 for ideas). If you cut pattern at shoulder line to make an asymmetric closing, stitch front pieces to back at shoulders, right sides together.

2 Sew Sleeves to Jacket body, right sides together, matching center of Sleeve edge with Jacket shoulder line.

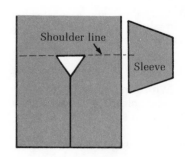

3 Fold garment in half at shoulder line, wrong sides together. On both sides, sew side seam and underarm seam as one.

Optional: Sew lining pieces, following steps 1–3. Baste to jacket, wrong sides together.

4 Stitch Neckband and Front band pieces together with a ¼-inch seam; press seam allowances open. Turn one long edge of band ¼ inch to wrong side; press.

5 Pin unfolded edge of band to jacket front edge with *right* side of band on *wrong* side of jacket; match neckband markings with shoulder lines. Stitch ¼ inch from edge. Press band and seam allowances away from jacket.

6 Fold band over onto right side of jacket and pin to jacket front just beyond stitching line; edgestitch.

7 Finish sleeve and hem edges with bias tape, following directions in "Encasing a raw edge" on page 33.

8 Make closing ties by cutting 4 strips of bias tape 8 inches long. Turn short ends ¼ inch to wrong side. Fold strip in half lengthwise with wrong sides together. Topstitch ⅛ inch from all edges. Evenly space ties at front closing and stitch just inside front band, as shown, above right.

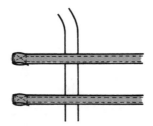

Optional: Buttons can be used instead of ties, but garment will fit a little more snugly. Position them at seamline of jacket and front band.

Making the vest

Note: If you don't line the vest, stitch flat fell seams (page 16).

1 Cut Vest as directed in Jacket Step 1, omitting Sleeves.
Optional: Cut lining piece; base to Vest, wrong sides together.

2 Cut 2 strips of bias tape—each 13 inches long for Size 1, 14 inches for Size 2, 15 inches for Size 4, 16 inches for Size 6. Matching center of bias tape to shoulder line, stitch bias tape to each Vest armhole. Follow techniques described in "Encasing a raw edge" on page 33.

3 Finish vest, following Jacket Steps 3–8.

Design: Stephanie Thompson of Mousefeathers.

[Pattern diagram: Front band Cut 2, Neckband Cut 1, Jacket back Cut 1, Shoulder, Jacket front, Sleeve Cut 2]

1 square = 2″ (For enlarging and transferring instructions, see page 38)
½″ seam allowance included

Pattern Size	Adjustment in Length	Width	Sleeve	Front Band
1	Subtract 1″ from both front and back lower edges	Subtract ½″ from each side edge (2″ decrease overall)	Subtract 1″ from upper sleeve edge	Subtract 1″ from band length
2	No change	No change	No change	No change
4	Add 1″ to both front and back lower edges	Add ½″ to each side edge (2″ increase overall)	Add 1″ to upper sleeve edge	Add 1″ to band length
6	Add 2″ to both front and back lower edges	Add 1″ to each side edge (4″ increase overall)	Add 2″ to upper sleeve edge	Add 2″ to band length

Toys & Accessories

Playthings, quilts, room decorations

The dolls, toys, quilts, and decorations in this chapter are designed especially for infants, toddlers, and preschoolers. The skill level required for making each project varies from novice (banners or hobby horses) to advanced (stenciled quilt or playhouse), but with a little time and patience, even the toughest can be tackled.

For most of the following projects, a reduced pattern appears on a grid. Enlarge the pattern, following the instructions in "How to transfer a design," page 38.

Stuffed accessories

Either pinned to clothes or worn as pendants, these easy-to-make shapes are sure to please.

You'll need . . .

Scraps of felt (*For star, use metallic fabric*)

Loose batting

Safety pin (*For lamb necklace, use ⅛-inch-wide ribbon*)

Sequins (*for fish, elephant, and cowboy boot*)

Pearl cotton (*for elephant, cowboy boot, and lamb*)

Glass beads (*for elephant and lamb eyes*)

2 buttons (*for race car*)

Pipe cleaner (*for lamb*)

Ribbon, 1½ inches wide (*for star*)

General directions

Refer to specific project instructions below before proceeding.

1 Transfer pattern to stiff paper (see page 38); cut along outlines.

2 Outline pattern pieces on fabric; *don't cut out shapes.* Place 2 pieces of fabric together, marked side up; stitch short stitches along marked outline, leaving an opening.

3 Trim fabric close to stitching. Stuff main shape with batting, and stitch closed.

4 Add features to front of shape. Whipstitch safety pin to back.

Fish. Before stuffing, complete decorative stitching on tail and fins; stuff body only. Whipstitch fin in place. Sew rows of sequins, working from tail to head. Use 1 sequin for eye.

Elephant. Glue decorations on saddle; outline hoofs with felt-tipped pen. For tail, cut three 1-inch pieces of pearl cotton; fold them in half and wrap at top with thread. Thread pearl cotton through tail top and insert ends (½ inch long) into opening in body; stitch opening closed. Complete decorative stitching around ear, and whipstitch ear in place. Sew on glass bead eye.

Race car. Complete decorative stitching on "exhaust," and shade as shown in photo, using a black felt-tipped pen; insert tab of exhaust into opening, and stitch opening closed. Glue on fabric number and stripes, and sew on button wheels.

Cowboy boot. Stitch contrasting-color stripe on front before stitching boot together. Fold narrow strip at top so that edge is caught in seam, forming a loop. With double strand of pearl cotton, attach sequin for spur, wrapping cotton around boot. Blanket stitch over cotton on instep.

Lamb. Using pearl cotton, sew bullion stitches (see page 27) on front before stitching lamb together. Use zipper foot to stitch around edge of shape. Before stuffing lamb, cut pipe cleaner in half; fold both pieces in half and insert them together into openings (as shown on grid) to form 4 legs and a double loop at the top. Stitch ears in place. Sew on beads for eyes. Add a stitch of thread for each nostril. Tack small bow to forehead. Thread 2 strands of ⅛-inch-wide ribbon through loop for necklace.

Star. Draw star on wrong side of metallic fabric. Place 2 pieces of fabric right sides together, and stitch around outline. Trim close to stitching, turn right side out, and stuff. Decorate with felt and ribbon.

Design: Phyllis Dunstan.

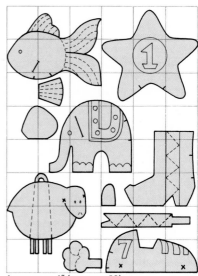

1 square = 1″ (see page 38)
Cut 2 of each piece
Leave opening between notches

Fold & carry crib

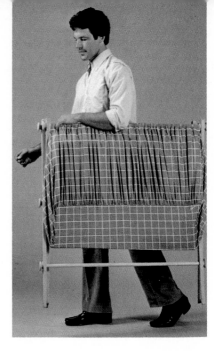

Portable and lightweight, this 36-inch crib allows you and baby to pick up and go—whether you're off to the beach or just to the back yard. Fabric handles make the crib easy to carry; a folding frame makes it easy to store in car trunk or closet.

You'll need . . .

4 1 by 2s, 4 feet long

5 ¾-inch hardwood dowels, each 36 inches long

10 2-inch wooden drawer pulls

10 2-inch #12 woodscrews

24 by 35-inch piece of ¼-inch plywood or tempered hardboard

Wood glue

4 yards medium-weight, firmly woven fabric, 45 inches wide

3½ yards ¼-inch nylon cord

24 by 35-inch foam mattress, 3 inches thick

1½ yards fabric (for mattress cover)

22-inch zipper

First the frame . . .

1 For each leg, make a 45 degree cut across one end of each 1 by 2. Measure from pointed end and cut boards 41 inches long. Starting at square end, mark each 1 by 2 at 2, 18½, and 32 inches. At each point, drill 3/4-inch holes for dowels. Sand to round off *square* ends only.

2 On each end of 4 dowels, place a drawer pull. Mark center, then drill hole through pull and dowel end for screw.

3 Connect two legs by running a dowel through bottom holes in 1 by 2s (angled ends of legs point same direction). Glue dowels into position; screw pulls to dowels. Repeat for other two legs.

4 Place frame halves together so legs cross at center holes, and angled ends of legs point outward. Cut two 1½-inch pieces of dowel. Glue one piece into *inner* 1 by 2 of each intersection, positioning dowel so one

end is flush with inside frame surface and other end projects toward other 1 by 2. Sand exposed dowel end to allow frame to pivot; don't glue outer 1 by 2s. Drill hole in pull and dowel, as in Step 2. Insert exposed dowel ends into outer 1 by 2s, and screw pull to dowel ends (see insert at right).

. . . Now the crib

1 Cut fabric pieces according to pattern and mark points for A, B, C, D, and E. Join Side pieces by matching A to A and D to D. Stitch right sides together ½ inch from edge.

2 Pin Slot Facing pieces along top edge at B, E, and C, right sides together. Mark slot; stitch along both sides of marking (see pattern). Cut slot. Turn Facing to inside; press and topstitch slot.

3 Turn under top edge of Side piece ½ inch, then 2½ inches, to make a casing. Stitch close to casing edge.

4 Gather bottom edge of Side piece (see "Gathering & stitching" on page 15) until markings on Side piece match Bottom piece. Pin and stitch Side to Bottom ½ inch from edge; stitch again ¼ inch from edge.

5 Stitch narrow ends of each Handle, right sides together, to make a loop. Press long edges under ¼ inch. Then fold Handle lengthwise, wrong sides together, so folded edges meet;

edgestitch. Stitch 1½ inches from bottom seam to make a loop for the dowel.

6 Insert dowels through casings from B to C, slipping Handle loop onto dowel at midpoints E.

7 Cut nylon cord in half. With each half make a 48-inch circumference circle; tie knot and trim excess. Feed cord loops through short ends of casing and slip loops over dowel ends.

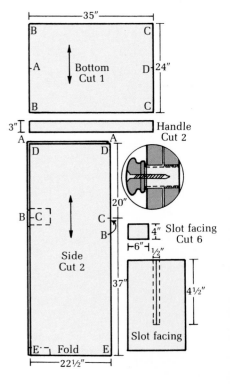

Fit dowels into frame; don't glue. Add pulls and screws, as in Frame Step 2.

8 Cut 2 pieces of mattress cover fabric, each 28¼ inches wide and 38 inches long. Placing right sides of fabric together, install zipper in one short side; open zipper a few inches. Keeping right sides together, stitch ½ inch from remaining edges. Open each corner and stitch across seam. Turn right side out through open zipper.

9 Mattress and board lie flat on bottom of bed. To close bed, turn mattress and board on their sides; fold bed frame and carry.

Design: Françoise Kirkman.

Alphabet quilt

Set aside several evenings to complete this project—you paint the stencils as you put the quilt together, and you must allow time for the paint to dry before continuing. This is a project for people with some sewing expertise.

You'll need . . .

For a 38½ by 48½-inch quilt:

4 yards neutral fabric (for quilt and backing)

⅝ yard rose fabric

¾ yard green fabric

2 yards polyester quilt batting

Thread to match neutral fabric

1 jar *each* of red, green, white, yellow, violet, and black fabric paint

#2 and #6 stencil brushes

Stencils: 1 package *each* 3, 2½, and 1-inch letters; 1 package 2½-inch numbers

Note: Our quilt was made with polished cotton. If you use this fabric, don't prewash—and don't machine launder the finished quilt. Dry cleaning is recommended to retain the fabric's polished appearance. If you're using plain cotton or cotton blends, do prewash all fabrics before starting your quilt.

Assembling the quilt

Note: Stitch all seams ⅜ inch from edge.

1 Mix all paint colors. For each, start with 1 teaspoon white, then add a little color. Seal with aluminum foil; store in refrigerator until ready to use. (For painting preparation and stenciling technique, see "Painting fabric," pages 52–55.)

Green = white, green, dash of red
Peach = white, red, yellow
Rose = white, red, dash of black
Lavender = white, violet

2 Cut rose fabric into 2½-inch-wide strips, green fabric into 5-inch-wide strips, from selvage to selvage.

3 Cut a 9 by 11-inch rectangle from neutral fabric. Mark guidelines on rectangle (see Diagram 2). Mark parallel lines 1½ inches from each guideline to create 1½-inch squares.

Stencil 1-inch letters in squares, alternating rose and peach colors. Let dry thoroughly; then heat-set (page 53).

4 From one green strip, cut four 5-inch squares; set aside. Using the rest of the strip, cut 1-inch-wide strips along crosswise grain. Fold 2 strips lengthwise, wrong sides together, and pin to short sides of rectangle; trim ends to fit. Baste ¼ inch from edge. These strips create a trimming, similar to piping but without a filler cord, between the center rectangle and rose strips.

5 Cut rose strips 1 and 2 (see Diagram 1) to fit short sides of rectangle. Pin to rectangle over green strips, right sides together; stitch. Turn rose strips right side up; press.

6 Trim two of the 1-inch-wide green strips to the length of remaining sides of the rectangle (not including rose fabric) plus ½ inch. Turn narrow edges of strips ¼ inch to wrong side; press. Fold strips lengthwise; center on remaining sides of rectangle (the strips won't extend to rose fabric). Baste to side of rectangle as in Step 4.

7 Cut rose strips 3 and 4 to fit long sides of rectangle; attach as in Step 5.

8 Cut batting and backing to fit rectangle; baste layers together. Machine quilt grid pattern in stenciled area; quilt rose strips in rows 1 inch apart. Refer to "Quilting," pages 48–51, for specific directions.

9 Cut 4½-inch-wide neutral strips 5–8, measuring length against rectangle. Cut out four 4½-inch squares and stitch to ends of strips 7 and 8. On strips, draw a guideline 1 inch from bottom edge; align bottom edge of letter on guideline. Using 2½-inch letters and green paint, begin and end stenciling ¾ inch from narrow edges. On each square, position a 2½-inch letter (see Diagram 3); stencil with rose paint. Let dry thoroughly; then heat-set.

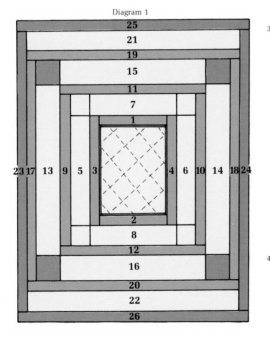

Diagram 1

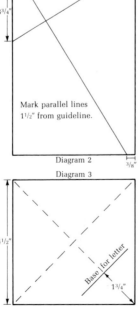

1⅛"   2¾"
3¾"
Mark parallel lines 1½" from guideline.
Diagram 2
⅜"

Diagram 3
4½"
Base for letter
1¼"

10 Cut and pin strip 5 to quilted piece, right sides together. Cut and add a backing strip, the same size as strip 5, right side against *wrong side* of quilted piece; stitch through all layers. Press strip 5 and backing away from quilt. Cut batting to fit between backing and quilt; baste layers together. Quilt ¼ inch from seamline. Repeat for strips 6–8.

11 Cut and stitch rose strips 9–12 (and their backing) to rectangle. Quilt in rows 2 inches apart. Quilt ¼ inch from seam on stenciled strips.

12 For strips 13–16, cut 5-inch-wide strips of neutral fabric the length of rectangle. Placing 3-inch letters on fabric as in Step 9, stencil

with lavender paint. Let dry thoroughly; then heat-set.

13 Stitch 5-inch green squares to both ends of 15 and 16. Add strips 13–16 as in Step 10. Add rose strips 17–20 as in Step 11.

14 For strips 21 and 22, cut 4½-inch-wide strips from neutral fabric the width of rectangle. Begin and end stenciling ⅞ inch from narrow edges. Use 2½-inch number stencils and alternate rose and peach. Let dry thoroughly; then heat-set. Add to quilt as in Step 10.

15 Use green strips for strips 23–26. Stitch right sides of strips 23 and 24 to wrong side of quilt; press

strips away from seam. Turn remaining edge of strips ¼ inch to wrong side; press. Cut batting 4½ inches wide and the length of strips; whipstitch one edge to seam allowance.

16 Fold strip and batting to right side of quilt, overlapping seam ⅛ inch; stitch strip close to edge.

17 Cut strips 25 and 26 two inches longer than quilt edges. Stitch strips to quilt with 1 inch extending at sides. Fold fabric edge and add batting as in Step 15. Fold 1-inch extensions to inside, then repeat Step 16. Blindstitch edges closed.

Design: Phyllis Dunstan.

Animals-on-parade quilt

Appliquéd animal figures march across a vividly colored patchwork quilt, charming any child and brightening any room. Fabric loops transform this quilt from crib cover to wall hanging.

You'll need . . .

For quilt 36 by 45 inches:

1½ yards red fabric, 45 inches wide

2 yards yellow fabric, 45 inches wide

⅔ yard turquoise fabric

½ yard *each* purple and green fabric

1 yard quilt batting, 45 inches wide

Thread to match each fabric color

⅔ yard fusible web, or glue stick (optional)

Making appliqué strips

Note: Preshrink and press all fabrics.

1 Enlarge pattern pieces according to grid scale (see page 38). Cut four of each figure, reversing one figure for elephant and hippo. Use yellow fabric for hippos, green for camels, purple for cows, and turquoise for elephants.

2 Cut four crosswise strips, each 7½ by 37 inches, from red fabric.

Space animals evenly on each strip, positioning reversed hippo and elephant as shown in photograph. Baste in place with fusible web or glue stick, or thread baste (see "Basting," pages 39–40).

3 With same color thread as animal, machine appliqué animals to fabric, following directions on pages 40–41.

Making patchwork strips

Note: Use ½-inch seams throughout.

1 Cut nine lengthwise strips, each 3 by 20 inches, from both the turquoise and the red fabric; cut nine lengthwise strips, each 3 by 15 inches, from both the green and the purple fabric.

2 Alternating colors, sew turquoise and red strips, right sides together, along long edges. Press all seams in same direction. Repeat for green and purple strips.

3 To make checkerboard strips, mark lines 3 inches apart across turquoise and red striped fabric. Cut on marked lines to make six 3-inch-wide strips. Reassemble strips in sets of two, reversing strips so colors and seam allowance directions are opposite; stitch. You now have 3 strips of fabric 18 squares long and 2 squares wide. Set aside.

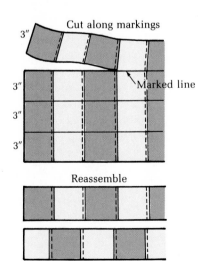

Cut along markings
3"
Marked line
3"
3"
3"
3"
Reassemble

4 To make triangle strips, mark and cut across green and purple striped fabric, making four 3-inch-wide strips. Sew all four strips, right sides together, to make a checkerboard pattern. Cut out triangle strips, including ½-inch seam allowances, following directions for "Triangle rows" on page 46.

Assembling the quilt

1 Cut 8 crosswise strips, 1½ by 37 inches each, of yellow fabric. Stitch patchwork and appliqué strips together in the order shown in photograph, stitching a yellow strip between each two patterned strips.

2 Cut batting same size as quilt face. Cut yellow backing 3 inches wider and 3 inches longer than quilt face.

3 Lay backing on flat surface with wrong side up. Center batting over backing; then place quilt face over batting, right side up. Baste layers together (see "Basting," page 49).

4 Machine quilt through seamlines that join appliquéd and yellow strips (see "Machine quilting," page 49).

5 Trim backing to extend 1 inch beyond each side of quilt face. Fold side edges of backing ½ inch to inside; press. Bring folded edge over quilt face, pinning it to quilt ½ inch from edge. Stitch through all layers close to pinned edge. Repeat with top and bottom edges. Stitch a square at corners, as shown.

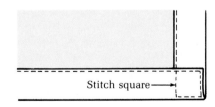

Stitch square →

6 Make dowel loops for wall hanging by cutting a strip of yellow fabric 2 by 16 inches. Fold strip in half lengthwise, right side out; press.

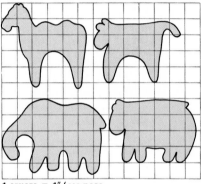

1 square = 1" (see page)

Open strip and fold long edges to wrong side, meeting at crease; then fold again along crease and press. Stitch close to edges. Cut strip into 4 equal pieces.

7 Stitch together short ends of one piece, ¼ inch from edge. Turn loop so seam is on inside at bottom of loop. Stitch across loop ¼ inch from edge with seam. Repeat for remaining strips. Space loops evenly across top of quilt; hand stitch in place.

Design: Karen Cummings.

Snuggly sock dolls

These soft, huggable dolls will spend many a night tucked in bed alongside your child.

You'll need . . .

For one dressed doll:

1 pair athletic tube socks with stripes (men's socks for *Big Sister*, boys' socks for *Baby Brother*)

12 ounces loose polyester filling

1 skein of 2-ply yarn

2 black ¼-inch shank buttons; 1 white ½-inch flat button

1 package red and white extra-wide double-fold bias tape

Fabric crayons in red, pink, and brown

8-inch length of twill tape

1 package cocoa brown liquid dye

Heavy-duty thread

For Big Sister's clothes:

½ yard red and white calico fabric

½ yard blue and white calico fabric

½ yard elastic cord

For Baby Brother's clothes:

¼ yard blue and white calico fabric

Scrap of white flannel fabric

Making the doll

Note: Stitch all seams in dolls with narrow zigzag stitch, close to edge.

1 Cut stripes off socks; set aside for *Big Sister's shoes*. Mix dye with water, according to manufacturer's directions. Dye socks a shade darker than desired skin tone.

Enlarge pattern pieces according to grid scale (see page 38). Transfer body piece outlines to socks and cut out.

2 Stuff Head. To shape face, insert balls of batting under cheeks and chin. To form nose, cover ½-inch flat button with sock fabric by taking small running stitches around edge of fabric, and pulling up thread to gather fabric, enclosing button; then place button inside head and press into batting, between cheeks. To make nostrils, bring threaded needle up inside head, through one hole in fabric-covered button, and out through face at nostril point. Catching a few sock threads with needle, push needle back into face, through button, and through head to back; secure thread at back of head. Repeat for other nostril.

3 Mark locations for eyes; color cheeks, mouth, and eyebrows with fabric crayons. Bringing threaded needle up through head, shape mouth by taking a tiny stitch at each end, pulling thread tightly to depress fabric; repeat at center, if de-

sired. Secure thread at back of head. Sew on button eyes in same manner, using heavy-duty thread.

4 Pin Arm seams, right sides together, and stitch, leaving top open. (Avoid overstretching material.) Turn Arms right side out. To make Legs, first cut, fold, and stitch slashes in Leg pieces, forming feet. Then stitch and turn, as for Arms. Stuff Arms and Legs, molding knees with balls of batting.

Turn Body inside out; pin Legs and Arms between Body front and back, and stitch. Turn Body right side out, stuff, and slipstitch shoulders closed. Turning raw edges under, slipstitch head to body.

5 *To make Big Sister's hair,* cut a 4 by 9-inch piece of cardboard; wrap yarn lengthwise around it 100 times, and cut yarn along one edge of cardboard. Measure back of head from forehead to neck, and cut twill tape that length. Center yarn over tape, spreading to cover length of tape. Press transparent tape over yarn and twill tape; stitch through all layers. Peel off transparent tape. Cut bangs at one edge, if desired; hand stitch hair through twill tape to center of top and back of head, using heavy-duty thread. Tie pigtails with bias tape, and tack bias tape to head.

For Baby Brother's hair, follow same procedure but use 4 by 4-inch cardboard. Pull random strands forward and tack in small bunches around face; trim short.

1 square = 2″ (For enlarging and transferring instructions, see page 38)   ¼″ seam allowances included

Making the doll clothes

1 Enlarge pattern pieces and cut out fabric. Also cut an 8 by 26-inch rectangle for Skirt of *Big Sister's dress*.

2 *For Big Sister's dress*, make narrow hems (see page 9) at center back edges of Bodice. Stitch Bodice front to back at shoulders. Make narrow hems at lower Sleeve edges. Measure and cut elastic for wrist, and tie a knot at each end. Zigzag stitch over elastic on wrong side of Sleeve, ¾ inch from edge. Gather Sleeve caps; stitch to armholes. Stitch side and underarm seams in one continuous seam.

Leaving a 2-inch opening at top, stitch Skirt back seam. Gather Skirt top and stitch to Bodice. Make a narrow hem at bottom of Skirt. Topstitch bias tape to neck edge (see page 34). Make a buttonhole and sew button at dress neck. Center and tack a 24-inch length of bias tape over seam between Bodice and Skirt, for sash.

For bloomers, turn bottom edges of legs under ¼ inch; turn again and stitch. Measure and tie one end of elastic; thread elastic through casings. Stitch leg seams, then stitch crotch seam. Repeat casing procedure for waist.

For Shoes, zigzag seams; turn right side out.

3 *For Baby Brother's Top*, stitch side seams. Topstitch bias tape to neck, hem, and armhole edges, extending tape 2 inches on each side at top of armholes to make ties.

For Diaper, turn fabric edges under ¼ inch; zigzag hem.

Design: Philippa K. Mars and Babs Kavanaugh.

Furry friends

How can you resist the beguiling character and soft, cuddly features of these two woodland friends? Both make wonderful companions for the young and young-at-heart.

You'll need . . .

For one stuffed animal:

- ½ yard fake fur (*for raccoon, gray; for bear, brown*)
- 1½ pounds loose polyester filling
- 2 round ½-inch-diameter buttons for eyes

  Scraps of synthetic suede (beige for *bear snout, inner ears, paw pads, and soles;* brown for *bear nose;* gray for *raccoon inner ears;* black for *raccoon nose and mouth*)

  10 by 10-inch piece of black fake fur (*for raccoon tail and mask*)

  ¼ yard firmly woven black fabric (*for raccoon hands and feet*)

Note: To cut fake fur, pin pattern pieces to wrong side of fabric; cut backing only, avoiding cutting into the pile. When stitching seams, push pile away from seamlines.

Making the bear

1 Enlarge bear pattern (solid-line pieces) according to grid scale (see page 38). Cut fabric pieces as directed on grid, adding ½-inch seam allowances. Reverse pattern pieces for Body Side, Head Side, and Snout Side to make left and right sides. Cut Snout Top, Snout Sides, Chin, Paw Pads, Soles, and 2 of 4 Ear pieces from beige suede. Cut a 2-inch circle for Nose from brown suede. Cut all other pieces from brown fake fur.

2 Stitch curved darts in Body Front; press toward center. Appliqué Paw Pads to arms on Body Front.

3 Pin and stitch Body Side pieces to Body Front, right sides together, leaving feet open at bottom edge. Stitch again to reinforce curves; clip curves. Stitch Soles to bottoms of feet, right sides together; clip curves.

1 square = 2" (see page 38)   Arrows indicate grainlines

Add ½" seam allowances to all edges

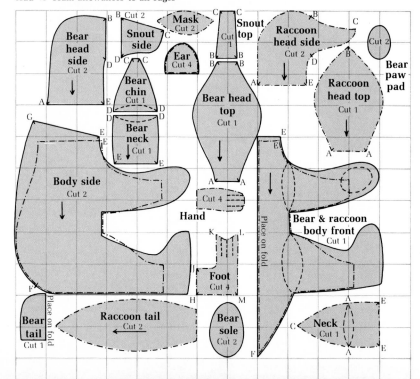

4 Stitch Body Side pieces, right sides together, along back seam.

5 To make head, stitch Snout Side pieces to corresponding Head Side pieces, and Snout Top to Head Top, right sides together, matching symbols. Stitch Chin and Neck together, then stitch curved dart in combined piece. With right sides facing, pin one Snout/Head Side piece to Chin/Neck piece, matching symbols; stitch. Repeat for other side. Then pin and stitch top Snout/Head piece in place. Clip curves and point; turn head right side out. Stitch darts in Nose; glue in place at tip of Snout.

6 With body wrong side out and head right side out, pin head to body, right sides together. Stitch, leaving back of neck open.

7 Turn bear right side out. Stuff body and head; slipstitch neck opening closed. Hand stitch button eyes in place.

8 Stitch inner and outer Ear pieces, right sides together, leaving bottom edge open. Clip curves and turn right side out. Turn raw edges under ½ inch; slipstitch Ears to head.

9 Fold Tail piece, right sides together; stitch curved side, leaving end open. Clip curves and trim seam. Turn right side out and stuff. Turn raw edges under ½ inch; slipstitch Tail to body at F.

Making the raccoon

1 Enlarge raccoon pattern (dotted-line pieces) according to grid scale (see page 38). Cut all fabric pieces *except Tail* as directed on grid, adding ½-inch seam allowances. Reverse pattern pieces for Body Side and Head Side to make left and right sides; reverse Hand and Foot patterns for 2 of the 4 pieces. Cut Hand and Foot pieces from black woven fabric; cut Mask from black fake fur. Cut 2 of the 4 Ear pieces from gray synthetic suede; cut Nose from black synthetic suede. All other pieces are cut from gray fake fur.

2 Stitch darts in Body Front; press toward center. With right sides together, stitch one Hand or Foot piece to each arm and leg on Body Front; repeat for limbs on Body Side pieces.

3 Pin and stitch Body Side pieces to Body Front, right sides together, leaving feet open between points K and L. Stitch again to reinforce curves; clip curves. To close each foot, bring raw edges together, matching seams in center; stitch across end.

4 Stitch Body Side pieces, right sides together, along back seam.

5 To assemble head, stitch Head Top to one Head Side piece, right sides together, matching symbols. Repeat for other Head Side. Stitch Head Sides together from B to C. Stitch curved dart in Neck, and then stitch to Head Side pieces, matching symbols. Clip curves and points; turn head right side out.

6 Follow Bear Step 6.

7 Turn raccoon right side out and stuff. Fill hands and feet first, then stitch fingers and toes along markings. Continue stuffing body and head; slipstitch neck opening closed.

8 Trim fur on snout close to backing; also trim Mask pieces. Machine zigzag along edge of Mask pieces; hand stitch them in place on face. Cut 2 by ¼-inch mouth from black synthetic suede. Hand stitch Nose, mouth, and button eyes to face.

9 Follow Bear Step 8.

10 To make Tail, cut five 9 by 2½-inch strips *each* of gray and black fur. Alternating colors, stitch them together with ¼-inch seams to make a 10 by 9-inch rectangle. Cut Tail pieces from rectangle. Stitch pieces, right sides together, matching fabric stripes. Clip point; turn Tail right side out and stuff. Turn raw edges under ½ inch; slipstitch Tail to body at F.

Design: Françoise Kirkman.

Learning toy: Lesson in a shoe

While playing with the Old Woman and her shoe, children can practice such skills as lacing, zipping, buttoning, tying, and snapping. Dolls of Mom and kids double as finger puppets for hours of absorbing imaginative play.

You'll need . . .

For one shoe house:

¾ yard blue felt

¼ yard gray felt

2 pieces black felt, 9½ by 11 inches

1 9 by 9-inch square *each* white, pink, red, brown, bright green, and dark green felt

⅜ yard polyester fleece

¾ yard craft-weight interfacing

1 package small appliqués of cherries

1 plastic separating zipper, 9 inches long

18 ¾-inch circles of nylon self-gripping fastener

2 red buttons, ¾ inch wide

1 large (coat-size) hook and eye

5 large sew-on snaps

10 hammer-on eyelets, ½-inch diameter

1 1½-inch buckle form

1 pair 38 to 40-inch shoelaces

Blue embroidery floss

Fabric glue or glue stick

Lightweight cardboard

For old woman and 6 children:

4 9 by 9-inch squares pink felt

Colored felt scraps

Yarn scraps

Black embroidery floss

Making the shoe house

1 Enlarge pattern pieces (see page 38). Transfer and cut as directed in steps below.

2 Cut 4 Side pieces from blue felt, 2 from fleece, and 2 from interfacing. Mark windows and door on one felt Side piece; transfer all other markings to same and one reversed felt piece.

3 With marked sides together, baste marked Side pieces, ½ inch from edge A; press seam open. Starting 1½ inches above bottom edge, install zipper in seam; stitch across top and bottom of zipper to secure to felt.

4 Spread zippered pieces on a flat surface, unmarked side up. Layer fleece, interfacing, then unmarked felt pieces on top (edges will overlap at center, over zipper); baste layers together.

5 On marked side, stitch just outside zipper stitching lines. On inside, cut the overlapping layers away from zipper area, close to stitching.

6 Topstitch sides through all layers, ⅜ inch from edges; trim fleece and interfacing from seam allowance between felt layers. Topstitch again, ⅛ inch from edges.

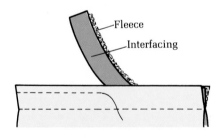
Fleece
Interfacing

7 Stitch along window and door markings. Stitch again ⅛ inch inside door markings. Cut out windows just inside stitching lines. Cut door between stitching lines along top, bottom, and right sides.

8 Cut two strips of red felt, ½ by 2 inches, for window boxes. Glue at bottoms of windows; stitch close to edges and across middle of each. Cut ¼-inch-wide strips of white felt for door trim; glue in place as marked; stitch close to edges of felt. Sew hook to door, eye to shoe, as door-fastening.

9 Cut tree and grass patterns from brown, dark green, and light green felt. Glue to plain Side; stitch in place. Glue and stitch cherry appliqués to tree.

10 Attach eyelets, as marked, to both front edges of Sides. Stitch red buttons and the loop halves of self-gripping fasteners to top edges, as marked.

11 Cut 2 Toe pieces from blue felt, 1 from fleece, and 1 from interfacing; transfer markings to one felt piece. Place marked felt piece on a flat surface, marked side down. Layer fleece, interfacing, then unmarked felt piece on top. Stitch as described in Step 6.

Stitch along window markings; cut out windows just inside stitching lines. Cut a red felt strip, ½ by 2¼ inches, for window box; stitch in place close to edges and across middle.

12 Cut two strips, 1 by 8½ inches, from blue felt; edgestitch strips together on long sides to make buckle strap. Pin strap to Toe at window, cutting edge at angle to fit; stitch in place. Cover buckle form with red felt. Cut a 1 by 6-inch strip of blue felt; fold in half and slip over buckle prong and center bar. Using a zipper foot, stitch across strip close to center bar. Attach free ends to Toe edge, as marked.

13 Transfer 3 long and 2 short Shutters onto white felt. Stitch along outlines through two layers of felt. Stitch horizontal lines with black thread, to make slats. Cut out shutters just outside stitching. Sew one snap half to back of each shutter and remaining half to shoe. Snap shutters in place.

14 Cut felt hearts, leaves, and numbers; glue to shutters and door.

15 Cut one Tongue from pink and one from blue felt; stitch together, ⅛ inch from edge. Sew tongue to toe at C, with edge of toe overlapping blue side of tongue ¼ inch.

16 Cut 2 Soles from blue felt, 1 from fleece, and 1 from interfacing; transfer markings to one felt piece. Place marked felt piece on a flat surface, marked side down. Layer fleece, interfacing, then unmarked felt piece. Stitch as described in Step 6. Then stitch marked lines across sole.

17 Place toe edges B over Sides, overlapping ¼ inch; stitch through all layers close to edge of toe. Pin top of shoe to sole, wrong sides together, matching center backs and center toes. Blanket stitch pieces together, using 6 strands of embroidery floss.

18 Cut one end off each shoelace; overlapping cut edges, stitch laces together. Lace shoe, starting from bottom. Tie at top.

19 Cut 2 Roof pieces from black felt. On one piece stitch the hook sides of 12 self-gripping fasteners, as marked. On the other piece, stitch the hook sides of 4 fasteners, as marked. Stitch Roof pieces together, with fasteners facing out, along short edges only. On roof inside (side with 4 fasteners), draw a line parallel to each short end, 1¾ inches from edge (you'll use these lines to position the roof ends). Fold Roof in half lengthwise, insides together, and press the crease.

20 Cut 4 Roof Ends from blue felt, omitting tabs from 2 pieces, for front gable. Cut 2 Roof Ends from interfacing ⅛ inch narrower on all edges; omit tabs on one of the interfacing pieces. Stitch layers together close to edges. Cut slits for buttonholes in tabs, as marked. Bind slit edges

(Continued on page 78)

. . . **Learning toy**

with a small blanket stitch, using 3 strands of embroidery floss.

21 Press roof-end flaps to inside. Pin *outside* of one flap to *inside* of roof, matching flap seamlines to marked line on roof, as shown; stitch through all layers. Repeat for remaining roof end.

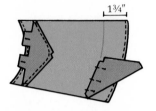

1¾″

22 Cut two pieces of cardboard, 4½ by 7½ inches. Slip into roof openings between layers of felt. Stitch close to lower edges of Roof.

23 Transfer Shingle outlines 6 times onto gray felt. Stitch along lines through two layers of felt, using small stitches; cut out just out-

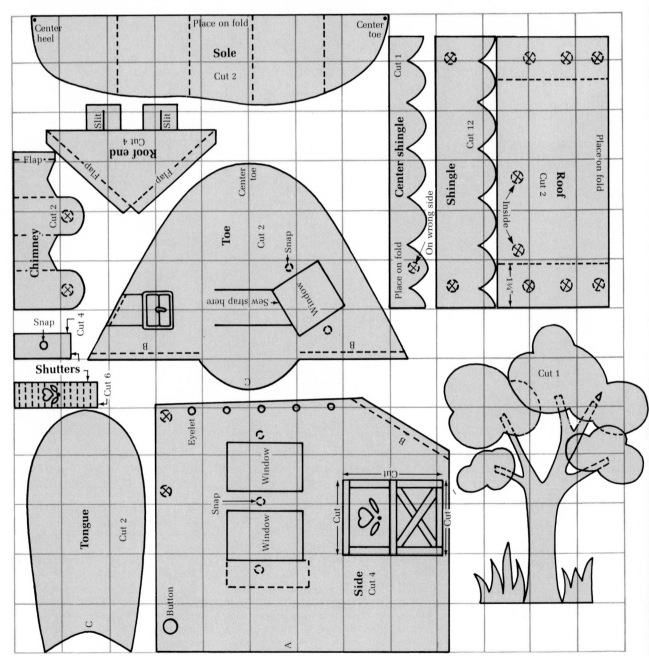

1 square = 2″ (For enlarging and transferring instructions, see page 38)
Seam allowances included where necessary.

side stitching. Stitch the loop side of a self-gripping fastener to each Shingle end, as marked.

24 Transfer Center Shingle strip onto gray felt; stitch along lines. Cut just outside stitching lines. At one end, stitch the hook sides of 2 self-gripping fasteners to outside, as marked. Glue center of underside to peak of roof.

25 Transfer Chimney onto red felt. Stitch along lines through two layers of felt. Then, with contrasting thread, stitch horizontal and vertical lines to make ¼-inch bricks above tabs. Cut out close to outline stitching. Stitch the loop sides of 2 self-gripping fasteners to inside of chimney tabs, as marked. Fold chimney on dotted lines; glue narrow flap to inside.

Making finger puppets

1 Enlarge patterns for Child and Old Woman. Trace patterns onto pink felt. Stitch on traced lines through two layers of felt, using small stitches; cut just outside stitching.

2 Cut eyes and cheeks from felt. (Optional: Use a paper or leather punch for perfect circles every time.) Embroider mouth with single strand of black floss. Glue eyes and cheeks in place.

3 Transfer clothing patterns onto felt scraps. Through two layers of felt, sew sides of dresses and sides and inside legs of overalls, on drawn lines. Cut out clothes just outside stitching and along lines; turn right side out. Dress each figure; slipstitch overall shoulders closed. Cut pockets and trims from felt scraps; glue in place.

4 In color to match each set of overalls, cut a 1 by 2-inch strip of felt; bring narrow edges together and stitch along raw edge. Tack to back of overalls for finger loop. Slip finger between girls' backs and dresses instead of making a loop.

5 To make each boy's hair, wrap yarn lengthwise around a 1¾ by 3½-inch piece of cardboard; don't overlap yarn when wrapping. Press tape over middle of yarn on one side of cardboard; slip yarn off cardboard. Keeping yarn flat, machine stitch down center of yarn, through tape and bottom layer of yarn; peel tape away. Sewing over first stitching, hand stitch yarn to center back of head, starting at forehead and ending at nape of neck. Cut yarn loops and trim to desired length. Apply glue to head to hold yarn ends in place.

6 To make each girl's hair, use a 1¾ by 5-inch piece of cardboard, and proceed as described above. Tie loose hair with ribbon, or braid hair.

7 For old woman's hair, use a bit of loose batting; glue in place.

Design: Phyllis Dunstan.

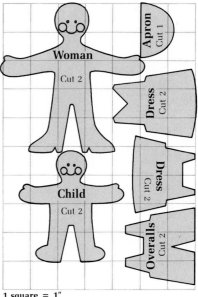

Woman
Cut 2

Child
Cut 2

Apron
Cut 1

Dress
Cut 2

Dress
Cut 2

Overalls
Cut 2

1 square = 1″

Child-size dolls

Lovably lifelike, these cuddly girl and boy dolls stand tall enough to wear toddlers' size 2 clothing—maybe their owners' hand-me-downs. Elastic foot loops link around a child's feet for dancing.

You'll need . . .

For one doll, 33 inches high:

1½ yards heavy unbleached muslin, 45 inches wide

1 package ½-inch elastic

2 white buttons, ½ inch in diameter

Felt scraps, black and white, for eyes

Felt-tipped pens or fabric crayons, for face

3 pounds loose polyester filling

Heavy-duty off-white thread

Cardboard

7½ ounces thick rug yarn (for girl's hair)

5½ ounces curly (bouclé) yarn (for boy's hair)

Making the doll

Note: Stitch ⅜-inch seams.

1 Enlarge and transfer patterns, including markings (see page 38). Fold muslin in half, selvage to selvage; cut out Doll pieces as indicated on grid.

2 With right sides together, making ¼-inch seams, stitch darts in Doll front and back. (Center dart in back of head joins 2 sides of Doll back.) Press all darts flat.

3 Stitch 2 Doll back pieces at center back seam, right sides together, leaving seam open between markings. With right sides together, stitch 2 pieces for each Arm, leaving upper end open. To reinforce, stitch again where thumb joins fingers. Clip seam allowance at wrist. Repeat for Legs, leaving seams open at toes (A-B-A) and at top of Leg. Stitch again to reinforce curve at ankle; clip seam allowances at ankle and back of knee.

4 With wrong side out, flatten toe area of each foot, folding at B and matching A's at center. Stitch across, B to A to B, to shape toe area.

Flatten each heel. Stitch across corner, as shown, to shape flat bottom of each foot.

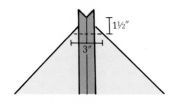

5 Turn Arms and Legs right side out. With filling, firmly stuff feet and calves of Legs; stuff thighs loosely. Stuff Arms firmly to within 1 inch of tops. Baste across tops of Arms and Legs to enclose filling.

6 With right sides together and raw edges even, place Legs between bottom edges of Doll front and back, making sure feet face forward. Stitch across bottom edge. Poke legs out through Doll back opening.

7 Baste Doll front to Doll back along sides and head; machine stitch as basted. Stitch again to reinforce curves at neck and waist; clip seam allowances. Cut slot in each shoulder, as marked. With thumbs facing up, insert Arms into slots, having right sides together and raw edges even. Check arm positions, then baste; machine stitch, using a zipper foot.

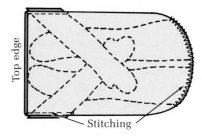

Stitching

8 Turn Doll right side out. Stuff with filling as firmly as possible. Hand stitch back opening closed with heavy-duty thread. Using same thread, hand stitch to shape fingers and toes. Wrap elastic to fit loosely around each foot. Stitch ends firmly to top of foot; then sew on small button, to cover ends.

9 For nose, cut a 2-inch (or smaller, if desired) circle of muslin. With heavy-duty thread, sew a running stitch ¼ inch from edge, to gather; stuff with tuft of batting, and pull stitches tight to shape nose. Slip-stitch to center of face. From felt scraps, cut 1-inch white circles for eyes and ½-inch black circles for pupils; appliqué or glue in place. Draw lips and brows, and tint cheeks, with felt-tipped pen or fabric crayon.

10 *To make hair for girl Doll:* Wrap rug yarn from top to bottom around 8¼ by 10¾-inch book or heavy cardboard until covered. Fasten yarn end, then hand stitch along one end of book to secure strands; cut yarn at opposite end, and remove book. Place stitched yarn on Doll's head with stitching line over center of head. Hand stitch over first stitching to hold in place. Fold yarn to one side, over stitching. Repeat procedure for other side of head. To

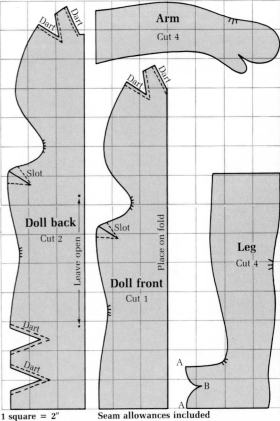

1 square = 2"   Seam allowances included
(For enlarging and transferring instructions, see page 38)

make bangs, repeat process, wrapping yarn around 3 by 5-inch cardboard and stitching along 5-inch side. Stitch bangs across forehead of Doll. Tie hair into 2 ponytails; tack to head.

11 *To make hair for boy Doll:* Wrap bouclé yarn around 3 by 10-inch cardboard, and hand stitch along one 10-inch side, as in Step 10. *Don't cut yarn;* slip looped fringe off cardboard. Stitch to head from side to side across forehead. Repeat the process, stitching overlapping rows of yarn fringe to head, from front to back, until head is covered.

Design: Françoise Kirkman.

Banners that blaze with color

Bold and brilliant, these banners brighten a child's room or wave from a window to announce a birthday. This grand-scale project is so simple that children can do it themselves.

Make the springtime or birthday banners shown on these pages, or dream up your own design for a special occasion—perhaps one like the summertime tree banner pictured on page 95.

You'll need . . .

For either painted banner:

1 jar *each* of violet, green, blue, red, yellow, and orange fabric paint

1 square foot of ½-inch-thick foam

Cardboard

#8 stencil brush

Small-blade art knife

Transfer pencil or dress-maker's chalk

For one birthday banner:

White, loosely woven cotton or cotton blend fabric, 38 by 72 inches

½ yard of wide ribbon

1 roll *each* of 4 or 5 colors of crepe paper streamers

Masking tape

Cardboard tubing, bamboo rod, or dowel, 42 inches long

For one springtime banner:

White twin-size flat sheet

Cardboard tubing, bamboo rod, or dowel, 56 inches long

Making the birthday banner

1 Turn all fabric edges under ¼ inch; press. Turn under again ½ inch, on sides and bottom; press. Machine stitch close to hem edges.

2 Enlarge star and heart designs, using grid scale (see page 38). Trace design outlines onto foam square;

cut out with art knife. Glue forms to cardboard backing to make stamps.

3 Outline freehand ribbon designs and lettering on fabric with transfer pencil (see photo at left). Use stencil brush to paint ribbons and lettering. (For preparation and painting instructions, see "Direct painting," page 52.)

Dip foam stamps into paint and press carefully onto fabric (see "Stamping," page 53). Allow to dry, and heat-set according to paint manufacturer's directions.

4 Turn under folded top edge 3½ inches and machine stitch close to hem edge, leaving side edges open. Insert tubing, bamboo, or dowel through hem opening.

5 Cut crepe paper streamers twice the banner's length. Fold in half and divide into two bundles, wrapping folded tops of each bundle with masking tape. Stuff taped ends into open ends of tubing, or tape to bamboo or dowel. Wrap ribbon around protruding ends of tubing, bamboo, or dowel.

Making the springtime banner

1 Trim sheet to 52 by 86 inches, making one hemmed edge the bottom edge of the banner. Turn unhemmed edges under ¼ inch; press. Turn under again 1½ inches on sides and press; machine stitch close to hem edges.

2 Enlarge butterfly and tulip designs, using grid scale (see page 38). Cut and mount foam forms as in Birthday Banner Step 2. Cut out separate forms for butterfly wings and body, so you can use contrasting paint colors for each.

3 Following Birthday Banner Steps 3 and 4, outline tulip stems, blue blocks, and border design with transfer pencil. Then paint and assemble banner.

Design: Julie Salles Haas.

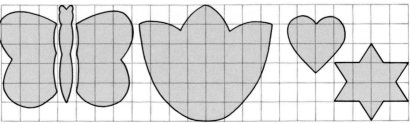

1 square = 1″ (For enlarging and transferring instructions, see page 38)

Inching upward chart

What happier way to celebrate a child's growth than with this colorful measurement chart? Besides marking off inches, it displays favorite photographs, from babyhood to the present.

As the child grows, change the pictures. Or use the frames to display locks of hair, report cards, or other memorabilia.

You'll need . . .

For one growth chart:

1¼ yards double-faced quilted fabric, 45 inches wide

¼ yard firmly woven fabric, for name and birth date

¼ yard firmly woven, heavy-weight, white fabric, 45 inches wide, for chart center

1½-inch-high letter stencils, for child's name

1-inch-high letter and number stencils, for birth date

1 measuring tape

Assorted pieces of fabric (6 inches square to 7 by 8 inches), for picture frames

Snapshots of child

Assorted trimmings (such as bias tape, braid, eyelet, lace, piping, ribbon, rickrack) for frames

1 yard heavy acetate, for windows

1 package wide bias tape, for hanging

1 dowel, 18 inches long, 1 inch in diameter

1 metal curtain rod or wooden slat, 18 inches long

Making the chart

1 From quilted fabric, cut a 21 by 45-inch rectangle. Cut a 1 by 2-inch rectangle out of each corner, as shown at top of facing page.

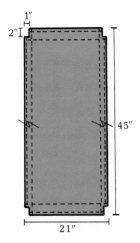

2 Mark front and back faces of quilted fabric (back folds over front to make border). Turn long edges of rectangle ½ inch to *front*; topstitch close to edge. Fold again 1 inch to *front*; topstitch ¼ inch from hem edge.

3 Turn top and bottom edges ½ inch to *front*; topstitch close to edge. Mark a parallel line across fabric *back* 2 inches from top and bottom folded edges.

4 Using 1½-inch-high letter stencils, cut child's name from fabric.

5 Place quilted fabric so that *back* is facing up and *top* edge is closest to you. Center letters of child's name between folded edge and marked line, with *base* of letters positioned *toward* folded edge. Machine appliqué letters in place (see page 40).

6 Using 1-inch-high letter and number stencils, cut child's birth date from fabric. Repeat procedure in Step 5, placing letters and numbers between bottom fold and marked line. Place *tops* of letters and numbers just below topstitching.

7 Cut a 9 by 38-inch strip from white fabric. Fold strip in half lengthwise, right sides together. Stitch long sides together, ½ inch from edge. Turn right side out; press flat, with seam at one edge. Center white strip on chart front; edgestitch in place.

8 Pin measuring tape 1 inch from left edge of white strip. Position tape so 20-inch line is at bottom edge of strip, and numbers increase going up the chart. Edgestitch along both sides of tape. Cut off excess tape at top and bottom.

9 Arrange pictures and assorted fabric squares and rectangles in vertical rows down chart sides. When arrangement is pleasing, mark position of each fabric piece on chart; make markings ½ inch narrower all around than fabric, to allow for hems in frames.

10 After deciding how much of each photograph you want to be visible, cut paper patterns to make a window for each frame. Cut a piece of acetate ½ inch larger on all sides than each window pattern.

11 Centering window patterns on right sides of fabric pieces, trace window openings. Stitch along traced lines; cut out window openings ¼ inch inside stitched lines. Clip corners to stitching, then press window edge under ¼ inch all around, along stitched lines.

12 Lay each frame on marked position on chart. On chart front, beneath frame pieces, mark openings to insert pictures, ½ inch above top edge of each window opening and ¼ inch wider than picture to be inserted. Stitch marked openings with buttonhole or zigzag stitching, as if making giant buttonholes, and slash.

13 Turn outer edge of frame ¼ inch to wrong side; topstitch. Embellish each frame as desired with ribbons or trims (see photo above).

14 Stitch acetate windows to backs of frames, close to window edge, catching the ¼ inch turned under in Step 11. Place frames on chart, making sure that each covers its slot. Topstitch frames to chart along all outside edges.

15 Cut 1½ yards of bias tape. Fold in half lengthwise; topstitch close to long edges; press.

16 Fold chart's top and bottom edges to front along marked line made in Step 3, forming 2-inch hems. Leaving side edges open, topstitch hems in place over ends of white center strip. In top hem, make tiny holes through all thicknesses, 2 inches from each end and ½ inch from top.

17 Slip pictures into their frames. Insert dowel through top hem, curtain rod through bottom hem. Thread bias tape through holes made in Step 16; stitch or tie ends together. Pull tape up from both front and back, to form doubled hanging loop. Hang chart so its lowest tape measurement reflects actual inch measurement from floor. With indelible ink, mark child's height on white center strip, next to measuring tape.

Design: Pamela Seifert.

Tooth fairy pillow

Deposit baby teeth in the Tooth Fairy's little moiré purse, then settle her down for the night. The next morning, peek inside—there should be a glint of silver in place of last night's ivory.

You'll need . . .

For one tooth fairy, 17 inches tall:

½ yard firmly woven ecru cotton or cotton-polyester blend fabric

¼ yard ecru moiré fabric

¼ yard heavy interfacing

Assorted ecru eyelet ruffle:
⅛ yard, 1 inch wide
½ yard, 2 inches wide
⅓ yard, 2½ inches wide
1 yard, 3 inches wide
⅔ yard, 4½ inches wide

Satin ribbon:
1 yard peach, ¼ inch wide
1 yard peach, ⅛ inch wide
1 yard tangerine, ⅛ inch wide

1 package ecru double-fold bias tape

1 pound loose polyester filling

1 skein bronze heavy rug yarn

Thread to match rug yarn

1 package each of brown, blue, and rose 6-strand embroidery floss

2 small circles of nylon self-gripping tape (optional)

Making the doll

Note: Use ½-inch seams unless otherwise indicated.

1 Enlarge and transfer pattern pieces (see page 38). With right sides together, fold cotton fabric in half, selvage to selvage; cut out Doll, Base, and two of four Purse pieces for lining. Cut two Wings and two Purse pieces from moiré fabric. Cut two Wings from interfacing. Transfer pattern markings to right side of fabric for Doll face, arm joints, and wing placement on Doll back.

2 Following markings, embroider brows and eye outlines in stem stitch with 3 strands of brown embroidery floss; use brown straight stitches for lashes, blue satin stitches for irises of eyes, and rose satin stitches for lips (see "Embroidery," page 26).

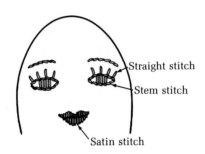

Straight stitch

Stem stitch

Satin stitch

3 Sew Doll front to back, right sides together, leaving bottom edge open; clip curves. Turn right side out.

4 Stuff arms with filling, from hands to elbow markings. Using zipper foot, machine stitch elbow joints as marked. Stuff remainder of arms to shoulder markings; stitch as marked to make shoulder joints. Turn doll wrong side out.

5 Sew Base panel to open end of Doll, right sides together, leaving a 4-inch opening in back for stuffing.

6 Turn Doll right side out. Stuff firmly with filling. Slipstitch opening closed.

7 For hair, cut 27 strands of bronze yarn, each 24 inches long. Attaching one strand with each stitch, use matching thread to hand sew centers of strands to center of head, forming a "part" from forehead to back.

8 Starting 2 inches from stitching at top of head, braid yarn hair on each side. Tack braids to side of head at neckline, then coil into a bun at back, following direction of arrows (following). Tuck braid ends under; tack braids and ends securely to head. Tack on small bows of ⅛-inch peach and tangerine ribbons.

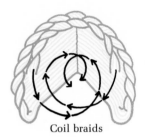

Coil braids

9 Place moiré Wing pieces right sides together. With both interfacing Wing pieces against wrong side of one moiré piece, pin together all 4 layers. Machine stitch layers together, ¼ inch from edge, leaving a 3-inch opening in one side.

10 Trim interfacing close to stitching; clip curves. Turn Wings right side out. Press, turning under raw edges of opening. Slipstitch opening closed. Topstitch close to outer edge of Wings. Stitch again ¼ inch inside first stitching. Whipstitch center of Wings to center back of Doll at marking.

11 Doll skirt is 5 overlapping rows of eyelet ruffle, each attached to Doll body. Measure distance around Doll, 4½ inches above base; add 1 inch for seam allowances. Cut 4½-inch-wide eyelet this length. With right sides together, join eyelet ends in diagonal seam, as shown, to form circular band. Slip band over Doll, then whipstitch in place.

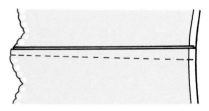

12 Repeat Step 11 with 4 remaining graduated widths of eyelet ruffle, each row overlapping the one below. (The second row overlaps the first by 2 inches; remaining rows overlap preceding rows by 1 inch.) For rows 2 and 3, use 3-inch-wide eyelet; for row 4, 2½-inch-wide eyelet; for row

5, 2-inch-wide eyelet. Leaving long ends free at center front, slipstitch ¼-inch peach ribbon over waistline edge of uppermost ruffle. Tie ends into a bow.

13 For collar ruffle, wrap 2-inch-wide eyelet around neck, folding top edge of eyelet at center front to make a V-shape. Fold under raw edges and whipstitch to center back, along Wing seam. Slipstitch ¼-inch-wide peach ribbon over top edge of ruffle. At center front, tack on bow of tangerine ribbon.

14 To keep hands joined, sew self-gripping tape circles to fingertips (pile circle on *outside* of one hand, hook circle on *inside* of other hand). Or simply stitch hands together permanently, *after* completing Purse.

15 To make Purse, match top edges of moiré and cotton Purse pieces, right sides together. Place 1-inch-wide eyelet between layers, with straight edges even. Machine stitch ¼ inch from top edge. Turn right side out; press.

16 Pin Purse with moiré sides together; sew side and bottom edge, ¼ inch from edge, including eyelet ends in seam. Secure seam ends with backstitching (for strength). Turn right side out.

17 Cut a 4-inch length of bias tape for Purse handle. Machine stitch long edges together. Hand sew ends of tape inside Purse at center front and back. (If doll hands are to be permanently joined, slip handle over arm before stitching hands together.) Decorate Purse center front with small bow of tangerine ribbon.

Design: Karen Cummings.

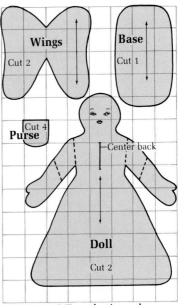

1 square = 2″ (For enlarging and transferring instructions, see page 38)

Arrow indicates lengthwise grain

Puppet menagerie

Stitch up this winsome quartet of furred and feathered characters, and then watch them come alive in the hands of delighted young puppeteers.

You'll need . . .

For one skunk or beaver:

⅜ yard medium-pile fake fur (for skunk, black; for beaver, brown)

Loose polyester filling

3 black dome-shaped buttons, ½ inch in diameter

5 by 36-inch strip of white, high-pile fake fur (for skunk gusset, tail, and stripe)

Scrap of red print fabric (for skunk's scarf)

Scrap of brown synthetic suede (for beaver tail)

Scrap of polyester batting (for beaver tail)

⅜ yard orange rib knit fabric (for beaver's cap)

1 white yarn pompon (for beaver's cap)

Scrap of white felt (for beaver teeth)

Scrap of corduroy fabric (for beaver ears)

For one chicken or parrot:

½ yard felt (for chicken, yellow; for parrot, red)

Loose polyester filling

2 black dome-shaped buttons, ⅜ inch in diameter

Fusible web

2 squares each of lavender, blue, turquoise, orange, and hot pink felt (for parrot)

1 square each of orange and rust felt (for chicken head)

Scrap of green calico fabric (for chicken's collar)

¾ yard green ribbon, ¼ inch wide (for chicken's collar)

Skunk or beaver

Note: When stitching seams, push pile away from seamlines.

1 Enlarge and transfer pattern pieces (see page 38), and cut fabric pieces following instructions on grid. For beaver, cut Body, Head, Gusset, and 2 of 4 Ear pieces from medium-pile fur; cut other 2 Ear pieces from corduroy. Cut Tail pieces from synthetic suede, and Cap from rib knit fabric. For skunk, cut Body, Head, and Ear pieces from medium-pile fur; cut Gusset, Tail, and Stripe pieces from high-pile fur; cut Scarf from red fabric.

2 Stitch Body pieces, right sides together, leaving bottom open. Clip curves; turn right side out. Turn hem under ¾ inch; topstitch. (For skunk, first sew Stripe to Body back with zigzag stitch along edges.)

3 Pin one Head piece to Gusset, right sides together, matching symbols; stitch from A to B. Repeat for other Head piece; stitch front head seam from A down to neck opening. Clip curves; turn and stuff.

4 Stitch Ears, right sides together, leaving bottom open. (For beaver, use 1 fur and 1 corduroy piece for each Ear.) Clip curves and turn. Turn edges under ¼ inch; slipstitch to head.

5 Pin Tail pieces, right sides together; stitch, leaving end open. Clip curves; turn. (For beaver tail, cut additional Tail piece from batting. Pin synthetic suede Tail pieces, right sides together; then pin batting piece against one suede piece and stitch through all 3 layers; trim, clip, and turn. Make bar tacks, as marked.) Stitch tail to back body at lower edge.

6 Turn lower edges of head under ¼ inch, and slipstitch to body with heavy-duty thread. Sew buttons in place for eyes and nose with heavy-duty thread. (For beaver teeth, transfer pattern to white felt; don't cut. Stitch on lines through 2 pieces of felt; cut Teeth out close to stitching, cutting halfway up between teeth at center. Slipstitch teeth to head.

7 For skunk's Scarf, turn edges under ¼ inch, turn again ¼ inch, and topstitch. For beaver's Cap, cut ear slits; fold Cap right sides together and zigzag stitch close to side edge. Fold bottom edge under ⅛ inch, and zigzag stitch hem.

Parrot

1 Enlarge and transfer pattern pieces (see page 38), and cut fabric

pieces following instructions on grid. Cut Body and Head from red felt; cut Wing, Chest, and Tail pieces from blue, orange, turquoise, lavender, and pink felt. Also cut corresponding Wing and Chest pieces from fusible web (cut web for Wing pieces A and B along dotted lines).

2 Arrange Chest pieces in order of descending size. Bond pieces to each other with fusible web; then bond chest to Body front along placement lines.

3 Pin Body pieces, *right* sides together, and stitch, leaving bottom open. Clip curves and turn. Stitch through both layers on wings following marked lines.

4 Arrange 3 large Wing pieces in order of descending size, matching edges at F; bond to each other and to wing backs on body with fusible web. Center smallest Wing piece D over edge F. Pin Tail pieces together in order of descending size, adding small Tail pieces E; machine stitch tail to bottom edge of body back through all layers.

5 Outline Beak pieces on orange felt; don't cut. Leaving straight sides open, stitch just inside lines through 2 layers of felt; cut out just outside stitching. Stuff beak loosely.

6 Pin beak to one Head piece at B-C. Pin Head pieces, right sides together, and stitch, leaving bottom open. Clip, turn, and stuff. With heavy-duty thread, slipstitch head to body, then sew on buttons for eyes.

Chicken

1 Enlarge and transfer pattern pieces (see page 38), and cut fabric pieces following instructions on grid. Cut Body and Head from yellow felt; cut Face pieces from rust felt. Also cut 2 Face pieces from fusible web.

2 Follow Parrot Step 3.

3 Follow Parrot Step 5, but do not stuff beak. Repeat process for Comb and Wattle pieces, outlining Wattle twice on felt.

4 Bond Face pieces onto Head pieces, as marked, using fusible web. Fold Beak pieces lengthwise, with upper beak overlapping lower beak, and folded edges facing away from each other. Pin folded *Beak,* plus *Comb* and *Wattle,* at marked locations on one Head piece, as shown. Then follow Parrot Step 6.

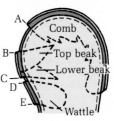

Chicken

5 To make Collar, cut a 14 by 5-inch rectangle of green calico. Turn short ends under ¼ inch, turn again ¼ inch, and topstitch. Fold fabric in half lengthwise, right sides together; stitch ¼ inch from raw edges. Turn and press; stitch ½ inch from seamed edge to form casing. Thread ribbon through casing; gather Collar around chicken's neck and tie ribbon in a bow.

Design: Philippa K. Mars & Babs Kavanaugh.

1 square = 2″ (For enlarging and transferring instructions, see page 38)   ¼″ seam allowances included

[Pattern grid with labeled pieces:]
- Skunk or beaver body — Cut 2, Fold
- Skunk or beaver gusset — Cut 1, Fold
- Chicken or parrot body — Cut 2, Fold
- Chicken or parrot head — Fold
- Skunk head — Cut 2
- Beaver head — Cut 2
- Parrot tail A — Cut 1, Fold
- Parrot tail B — Cut 1, Fold
- Parrot tail — Cut 1, Fold
- Parrot tail — Cut 2
- Skunk tail — Cut 2, Fold
- Ear — Cut 4
- Beaver tail — Cut 2, Fold
- Teeth — Cut 2
- Parrot wing D — Cut 2
- Parrot wing — Cut 2
- Parrot wing A — Cut 2
- Parrot tail — Cut 1
- Parrot chest A — Cut 1, Fold
- Parrot chest B — Cut 1, Fold
- wattle — Cut 4
- Parrot chest C — Cut 1, Fold
- Chicken face — Cut 2
- Chicken top beak — Cut 2
- lower beak — Cut 2
- E — Cut 2, Parrot tail
- Parrot tail — B
- Beaver cap — Cut 1, Slit for ear
- Chicken comb — Cut 2
- Skunk scarf — Cut 1, Fold
- Skunk stripe — Cut 1
- Parrot wing B — Cut 2
- Parrot wing C — Cut 2
- Parrot beak

Beanbag buddies

Comfy to curl up in, sturdy enough for a bouncy ride, our ring-necked mallard and bright red hen quickly become favorite friends.

You'll need . . .

Note: Use firmly woven cottons or cotton blends, 45 inches wide.

For one beanbag hen:

4½ yards red and white print fabric

¼ yard red fabric

Scraps of white fabric

5 pounds loose polyester filling

7 cubic feet (2½ bags) styrene foam pellets

Heavy-duty thread

For one beanbag duck:

1 yard dark green fabric

¾ yard white fabric

½ yard each yellow and black fabric

1¾ yards red and white print fabric

1½ yards red fabric

Scraps of white fabric

6 pounds loose polyester filling

7 cubic feet (2½ bags) styrene foam pellets

Making the hen

Note: Stitch ½-inch seams.

1 Enlarge and transfer appropriate pattern pieces (see page 38) and markings (ignore dashed lines on Body Top, Body Side, and Underbody). Cut Head, Beak Gusset, Neck Circle, and Body pieces from print fabric; Comb and eye pupils from red fabric; and eyes from white scrap.

2 Machine appliqué eye and pupil in place on each Head piece. With right sides together, stitch 3 Comb pieces in place on each Head piece; press seams open.

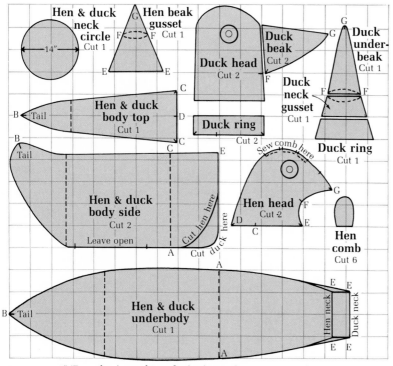

1 square = 5" (For enlarging and transferring instructions, see page 38)
½" seam allowances included

3 Folding right sides together, stitch curved dart F in Beak Gusset. Matching E, F, and G, stitch one edge of Gusset to each Head piece, right sides together. Clip curve. Matching Comb pieces, right sides together, stitch 2 Head pieces along top curved edge, leaving straight edge (neck) open. Clip curve and corners; turn right side out.

4 Firmly stuff Head with filling, poking in small amounts at a time. When Head is packed full, place Neck Circle over neck opening, wrong sides together, matching edges. Use zipper foot to stitch neckline seam, enclosing stuffing.

5 Stitch Body Top to each Body Side, right sides together, matching B and C; clip curve. With right sides together, matching E, A, and B, stitch Underbody to remaining edges of Body Sides, leaving 10 inches open in one straight side. Clip curves. In-

sert Head (upside down, beak forward) into neck opening. Matching D and E, use zipper foot to stitch over Neck Circle. Turn hen right side out.

6 Have someone hold hen open, and fill with pellets, using funnel of heavy paper to fill completely. Carefully pin opening closed. Hand stitch closed with heavy-duty thread.

Making the duck

Note: Stitch ½-inch seams.

1 Enlarge and transfer appropriate pattern pieces (see page 38). Separate pieces as indicated by dashed lines, adding ½ inch to these edges for seam allowances. Cut Tail portions of Body pieces from black fabric; Center Body portions from print; Front Body portions from red; Head,

Neck Circle, Neck Gusset and eye pupils from green; Ring from white; and Beak, Under-beak, and eyes from yellow.

2 Stitch Under-beak to Neck Gusset, right sides together, making curved seam F as marked. Stitch remaining long Gusset edge to matching edge of Neck Ring piece, as positioned on grid. Press seam open. Stitch Beak and Ring pieces to Head pieces, as positioned on pattern. Press seams open. Appliqué eyes and pupils as in Hen Step 2.

3 Join Under-beak/Gusset piece to each Head side as in Hen Step 3; then finish head as in Hen Step 4. With right sides together, making ½-inch seams, piece patchwork sections of Body Top, Sides, and Underbody. Press seams open. Finish duck as in Hen Steps 5 and 6.

Design: Françoise Kirkman.

Tender-hearted bear quilt

Loving hearts float upward from baby's bear. A charming wall hanging, it's also a cozy crib-size quilt.

You'll need . . .

For 1 quilt, 35½ by 44½ inches:

1⅔ yards firmly woven cotton or cotton blend print fabric, 45 inches wide

1 yard navy fabric, 45 inches wide

¾ yard green fabric, 45 inches wide

½ yard brown fabric, 45 inches wide

¼ yard beige dotted fabric

¼ yard mauve dotted fabric

1 yard quilt batting, 45 inches wide

Size 5 pearl cotton: 1 skein *each* in black, yellow, and each fabric color

Assembling the quilt

1 Enlarge pattern pieces according to grid scale (see page 38), adding ¼-inch seam allowances, and trace on wrong sides of brown, beige, and mauve fabric, following photograph for color placement; cut out pieces.

2 From print fabric, cut a 20½-inch square for quilt center. Curve corners, using pattern. Arrange bear pieces and 2 smaller hearts on square; baste in place (see page 39). Hand appliqué with matching pearl cotton (see page 41). Satin stitch bear's eyes with yellow pearl cotton, and nose with black. For mouth, use a running stitch and black pearl cotton (see page 26).

3 From green fabric, cut a 26½-inch square; curve corners, as in Step 2. Center print square over green square; appliqué in place. Turn piece face down. Carefully cut away green fabric, stopping ½ inch from appliqué stitching. On right side, appliqué remaining heart in place.

4 From navy fabric, cut a 45 by 36-inch rectangle. Center appliquéd square over it. Appliqué green fabric edge to navy fabric. Carefully cut away navy fabric, as in Step 3. Press.

5 Mark diagonal quilting lines 4 inches apart on navy border (see "Quilting," pages 48–51). Cut print fabric backing piece and batting the same size as finished quilt face.

6 Assemble and baste quilt layers (see page 49). Quilt along diagonal lines and all appliquéd edges.

7 Following directions in "Cutting bias strips," page 32, make 1½-inch-wide bias tape from print fabric. Bind quilt edge with bias (see page 33).

Design: Sonya Barrington.

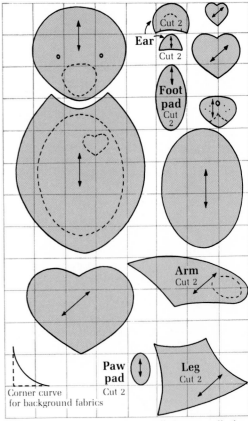

Ear — Cut 2 / Cut 2

Foot pad — Cut 2

Arm — Cut 2

Paw pad — Cut 2

Leg — Cut 2

Corner curve for background fabrics

Cut 1 unless noted   Add ¼″ seam allowance to all edges
1 square = 2″ (see page 38)

Hop-along hobby horses

Either of these horses, or your own variation, is sure to "whinny" its way into your child's heart.

You'll need . . .

For one horse:

⅓ yard low to medium-pile fake fur

20 by 4-inch strip high-pile fake fur

½ pound loose polyester filling

2 large and 2 small half-dome buttons

Heavy-duty thread

White glue

3-foot dowel, ⅜ inch or ½ inch in diameter

Scrap of corduroy (*for horse ears*)

⅛ yard gold lamé (*for unicorn horn*)

Assembling the horse

Note: When stitching fake fur, push pile *away* from seams.

1 Enlarge and transfer pattern pieces (see page 38). Cut Head, Gusset, and Ears from low-pile fabric. (*For horse*, cut 2 of 4 Ears from corduroy.) Cut Mane from high-pile fabric. (*For unicorn*, cut Horn from gold lamé.)

2 Stitch Head pieces, right sides together, from A down to neck edge. Pin and stitch Mane to Gusset at B. Pin Gusset/Mane to one Head piece; stitch from A to C. Repeat for other Head piece. Turn right side out and stuff head above neck.

3 Slipstitch one seam joining Mane to head below C. Stuff neck except for bottom 2 inches. Insert dowel in neck; spread glue inside neck. Bring remaining seam edges together. Wrap heavy-duty thread around neck to secure it to dowel; let dry. Slipstitch remaining seam closed.

4 Stitch each pair of Ears, right sides together, leaving lower edge open. (*For horse*, use 1 fur and 1 corduroy piece for each ear.) Turn right side out; slipstitch to head.

For unicorn, stitch Horn pieces, right sides together; turn and stuff. Slipstitch Horn to head.

5 Sew large buttons in place for eyes; use small buttons for nostrils. If desired, add bridle of ½-inch-wide ribbon, neck scarf, or fake flowers.

Design: Philippa K. Mars and Babs Kavanaugh.

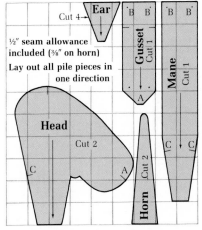

1 square = 2″ (For enlarging and transferring instructions, see page 38)

Miniature dream cottage

Transform an ordinary card table into this charming playhouse, complete with see-through windows and cheery appliquéd garden. This project is recommended for those with sewing experience.

You'll need . . .

- 1 card table, 34 by 34 inches
- 2 sheets corrugated cardboard, 36 by 72 inches
- 2 yards quilted blue fabric, 45 inches wide, for roof
- 4½ yards heavy blue corduroy, 45 inches wide, for walls
- 1½ yards white corduroy
- 1½ yards red corduroy
- ½ yard purple corduroy
- ¼ yard *each* light green and dark green corduroy
- 12 yards red extra-wide double-fold bias tape
- 1½ yards heavyweight acetate
- 1 spool thread for each fabric color
- ½ yard nylon self-gripping fastener tape

Making the house

1 To make cardboard roof, measure, mark, and cut one Gable and one Roof from *each* sheet of cardboard, following layout above right. (Also cut Gable pattern [minus tabs and flaps] from paper, to use later). Using metal straightedge and utility knife, score cardboard along dotted lines; fold. Matching center X's on Roof, securely tape Gable tabs and

flaps to underside of one Roof. Tape second Roof to underside of first.

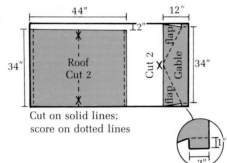

Cut on solid lines; score on dotted lines

2 Cut Roof fabric 40 by 45 inches. Lay wrong side up over Roof form, leaving a 3-inch overhang over each Gable. Pin darts to fit fabric snugly at 4 corners and 2 Gable peaks. Remove from form; stitch darts as pinned. Turn all outer edges under ½ inch; topstitch ¼ inch from edge.

3 To cut out Front Wall from blue corduroy, center paper Gable pattern across width of fabric. Extend slanted roof lines to selvages with chalk or pencil. Measuring 24½ inches from bottom edge of Gable pattern, mark bottom line across fabric. Cut out piece on roof and bottom lines. Turn bottom edge under ½ inch, turn again 1 inch and pin; turn side edges under 5 inches. Topstitch close to all hem edges. Center and cut 12 by 21-inch opening for Door.

4 To trim Door opening, cut 5-inch-wide strips from white corduroy; piece into a 2⅛-yard length. Fold

long edges under ½ inch; press. Fold strip lengthwise, wrong sides together, aligning folded edges; press. To attach trim, start at bottom edge of opening, turning narrow edge of strip under ½ inch; pin strip over raw edge of Door opening with inside of fold against edge of opening. To turn corners, make a mitered corner on front and back sides of trim. Stitch trim to wall through all layers, ¼ inch from trim edge.

5 Cut tulip shapes from purple corduroy, stems and leaves from dark and light green corduroy, and numbers from white corduroy; appliqué to wall (see page 39). If desired, stitch mailbox of blue corduroy.

6 For Front Door, cut red corduroy 19 by 26 inches. Turn bottom and sides under ½ inch; turn again 1½ inches, and topstitch close to hem edge. Mark a 10-inch-radius semicircle for window, cut out opening, and bind edges with bias tape (see "Bias tape," page 32). Cut acetate slightly larger than opening; stitch folded bias tape "spokes" to acetate. Center acetate on wrong side of window opening and stitch to Door, close to window edge.

7 Cut cat and doorknob shapes from dark green corduroy; appliqué to Front Door. With all bottom hems even, pin and stitch finished Door across top of Front Door opening, against *inside* of trim.

8 To make Back Wall, mark, cut, and hem blue corduroy (see Step 3). Cut out 20 by 21-inch Back Door opening, as for Front Door. Cut 5 inch by 2½ yards long white corduroy strip for trim; trim Door opening (see Step 4).

9 For Back Door (see photo), cut red corduroy 27 by 25 inches. Cut two 7 by 14-inch window openings centered on door. Bind openings with bias tape (see page 32). Cut a 23-inch-square piece of acetate. Matching tops of acetate and corduroy, mark window openings on acetate. Stitch bias tape to acetate to form window panes; stitch acetate to wrong side of Door around window

openings. Hem sides and bottom; stitch Door to wall (see Step 6).

10 Cut one Side Wall, 27½ by 45 inches, from blue corduroy; hem (see Step 3). Center and cut out a 9½ by 11½-inch window opening (see photo, facing page). Cut 5-inch wide by 2¼ yards white corduroy trim; trim opening as for Door in Step 4.

11 To make window, cut acetate 14 by 16 inches. Draw outline of window centered on acetate. Press bias tape open; stitch to acetate centered along outlines. Stitch folded tape to acetate to form window panes. Center acetate on wrong side of window opening; edgestitch to white trim, ¼ inch from trim edges.

12 Make Shutters from 2 pieces of white corduroy, *each* 9½ by 25 inches. Turn all edges under ½ inch; press. Matching short edges, fold each piece in half, wrong sides together; edgestitch ¼ inch from all edges. Stitch self-gripping fastener tape to each Shutter at top corner, front and back; stitch matching pieces on house wall, and above window (see photo). Stitch Shutters to window's sides. Add tulip appliqués to wall below window (see Step 5).

13 Cut out and hem remaining Side Wall (see Steps 3 and 9). Add pockets made of scraps or nylon netting fabric to inside of wall, if desired.

14 With fabric roof in place on table, pin walls evenly to roof edges so hems touch floor; overlap wall panels at corners. Remove from form; stitch walls to roof on all sides with 2 rows of stitching ¾ inch apart.

Design: Pamela Seifert.

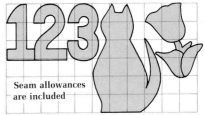

Seam allowances are included

1 square = 2" (For enlarging and transferring instructions, see page 38)

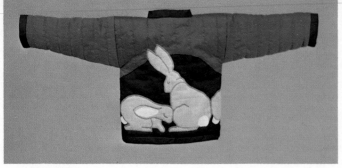

Index

Machine-appliquéd bunnies (photos above) or apples (below) make these garments one of a kind. Use the "Wardrobe toppers" pattern on pages 62–63 for the jacket and vest. The appliqué patterns appear on page 43.

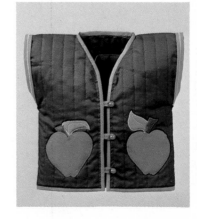